Perspective Rendering for the Theatre

Books on Stagecraft

Drafting for the Theatre
Dennis Dorn and Mark Shanda
Imaging the Role: Makeup as a Stage in Characterization
Jenny Egan
Stage Rigging Handbook. Second Edition
Jay O. Glerum
Sceno-Graphic Techniques. Third Edition
W. Oren Parker
Computer Scenographics
Darwin Reid Payne
Theory and Craft of the Scenographic Model
Darwin Reid Payne
Perspective Rendering for the Theatre
William H. Pinnell
Theatrical Scene Painting: A Lesson Guide
William H. Pinnell

Perspective Rendering for the Theatre

William H. Pinnell

Southern Illinois University Press • Carbondale and Edwardsville

99   98   97   96   4   3   2   1

Library of Congress Cataloging-in-Publication Data

Pinnell, William H.
   Perspective rendering for the theatre / William H. Pinnell.
      p.   cm.
   Includes bibliographical referencs (p.   ) and index.
   1. Theaters—Stage-setting and scenery.   2. Computer-aided design.
3. Perspective.   I. Title.
PN2091.S8P49   1996
792'.025—dc20   95-45512
ISBN 0-8093-2053-3 (pbk. : alk. paper)   CIP

The paper used in this publication meets the minimum requirements of
American National Standard for Information Sciences—Permanence of Paper
for Printed Library Materials, ANSI Z39.48-1984. ♾

For Tara and Bobby

Contents

Acknowledgments

My sincere appreciation is extended to project editor Teresa White and copyeditor Tracey Moore for their professional talents and extremely helpful attention to detail. And, lastly, I wish to thank Kelly for her love and constant encouragement.

Perspective Rendering for the Theatre

1. Introduction

This is not a book on theatrical design but rather a treatise on one particular method of how to *convey* a design. Whether one wishes to construct a model of a stage setting or to illustrate a design by means of a color rendering, either method of presentation should accurately reflect what will eventually appear on the stage.

Theatrical design is not meant to be a literal art form. Most people do not wish to attend the theatre in order to be reminded of their own existence or personal circumstances. While good theatre should provoke thought and a certain degree of analysis, entertainment remains the primary reason why people attend. For the brief time they are nestled in their seats, people wish to experience an event and perhaps visit a place that could exist only in the imagination. What was moments before a dark, cavernous room quickly becomes an intimate personal voyage illuminated by magic and light. Robert Sherwood spoke for the audience when he said that "theatre is the dwelling place of wonder." To a very large degree, the stage setting provides the primary visual support for that place of wonder, since it is the environment for the action of the play's events.

Stage design can be realistic in nature and is often expressed (perhaps all too frequently) in authentic, naturalistic terms. But, thankfully, much design for the theatre attempts to capture moments and locales in surreal, expressionistic, or abstract ways so as to create a setting for the circumstances and conditions that are unique to that play's message or character's plight. The stage setting must not be universally applicable to many plays but must strive to be appropriate to one particular play's life. An outdoor scene in which a balcony is viewed, for example, does not automatically qualify that set to serve appropriately the dramatic needs of both *Romeo and Juliet* and *Cyrano de Bergerac*. Though the physical requirements of these two balcony scenes are quite similar, the designer must always strive for a definitive visual interpretation. In essence, what should be conveyed is a moment in time, not merely an arena that is capable of housing any number of events. As such, through this uniqueness of expression, the setting takes pains to underscore and support the play script and, in so doing, is sometimes manifested in stylized form, line, texture, or color.

The scenic designer communicates his or her ideas through a series of initial sketches that, through directorial consultation, eventually evolve into the finalized, approved plans for the actual setting. A large quantity of these plans take the form of working drawings, for example, floor plans and elevations, and the related schematics necessary for the shop staff to construct the design. But perhaps the most integral part of these plans will be the colored indication of how the set will appear when completed. This colored indication commonly takes one of two forms: the **rendering** or the **scenic model**. To many involved in the production, the rendering or scenic model is the single most significant contribution to the planning stage of the production.

Regardless of the nature of scenic intent or the direction it may take, the designer's *communication*, through either the rendering or model, is best achieved when done literally. That is to say that the style of the setting has no bearing whatsoever on the realistic way it should be communicated. What one sees when one looks at a model of a set is, to the closest approximation, what one will see when that set eventually appears on the stage. The model's spatial proportions, positioning, texture, and color should be a scaled-down representation that faithfully and accurately depicts the full-size finished set. Otherwise what would be the point of the model? The designer does not say "picture this," but rather allows the scenic model to speak on his or her behalf in a tangible, realistic way. The style of the design may not be realistic, but its *communication* must be in realistic terms.

Why should the same acuities of communication and perception not be the guidelines for the designer's rendering? With the model, "what you see is what you get." Rightfully, the designer who chooses to do a rendering instead of a model, for whatever reasons, should be bound by the same fidelity of conveyance: to illustrate the truth of what will be realized onstage.

Exemplary renderings by some of the finest scenic designers are indeed works of art. And, true to the tenets of design responsibility, their renderings are powerfully evocative and their quests to capture mood and moment are astoundingly moving. But what is at issue here is the matter of whether some of these renderings picture (1) what is intended, or in fact, (2) what will be realized. Ideally, the two should be the same; commonly, there may be a world of difference between the two.

The intent to accurately picturize what will occur on the stage is what this book is meant to address: How does one, by means of a theatrical rendering, faithfully represent how the actual, finished stage design will appear?

The obvious solution to this task would be forget about a rendering and, instead, learn to build and paint a scaled model. After all, the model has the advantage of becoming the pictorial equivalent of not one rendering, but many. By changing the viewer's position, innumerable views can be obtained. By the very nature of its three-dimensional form, it is more spectacular than a perspective rendering. The model is constructed so as to give a verisimilitudinous representation that, from this standpoint, gives it a great superiority over the perspective rendering. Another element that strengthens the case for a model is that most theatrical directors prefer and have come to rely on a model for their thorough understanding of the setting.

But making the perspective rendering does have some advantages, among them cost, space, size, duplication and time. First, while a model can be quite expensive to construct, the cost of creating and matting a rendering is comparatively economical. Secondly, while the construction and painting processes involved in model-making require a considerable amount of work space, the rendering can be drawn and painted at the drawing board. The rendering also has the advantage of being compact enough to slip into a portfolio case for ease in portability. In addition, impressive, multiple copies of the rendering can be made by laser-copy printing; alternately, one would have to photograph a view of the model and have prints made for distribution. Although a photograph could be made, the process is hardly as efficacious as a laser print. Time is another factor. It usually takes considerably longer to construct and paint a model than it does to draw and paint a rendering. Finally, perspective renderings can be painted so as to illustrate how the completed stage setting will appear when under stage lighting. The rendering is, after all, an accurate illustration of a theatrical moment, not simply a miniaturized version of the actual setting.

One might argue the point for using a CAD (computer-aided design) program. Truly, not only can such programs make tasks of picturization easier, but they can counteract human error and retrieve incredible amounts of data for design consideration. Once entered into the system, data can be modified, discarded, or stored for recovery at will. CAD programs bridge the differences between scenic models and renderings, since computer-created perspective can generate multiple viewpoints and allow the observer to change an angle of sight (or point of observation) without getting out of a chair. Colors can be chosen from a computer range involving several thousand variations of hue. There are, of course, drawbacks to CAD as a method of picturization. Although the individual free-lance designers might find working with CAD initially quite exciting, keeping abreast with technological developments and innovation could well become a full-time job.

Using CAD might also prove technically and economically inadvisable. A scenic designer's finalized designs and accompanying plans, by the very requirements of established theatrical scale, normally result in fairly large and often intricate drawings. As if the complexities of programming the necessary information into the computer were not enough of a task, the printing of the verified drawings also requires a **plotter**, a machine far more advanced than the average printer. The plotter is a mechanism that enables a pen to glide along the paper and actually draw the various images fed into it by the computer. Consequently, the plotter must be at least as large as the drawings themselves. From an economic standpoint, the computers and plotters that can generate perspective and other related sophisticated graphics require expensive, powerful software. The more thorough and convincing the visual requirement, the more intricate and costly the equipment. Sizable computer-generated graphic capabilities only come with sizable investments. If the work projects are not sufficient in number to justify the cost of the operation, then working with CAD will simply not be a reality for most individual designers.

Though graphic computer systems, large or small, may greatly assist the designer in preparing perspective drawings, the computers can only react to the information and directions input by the operator. To ask the computer to perform a particular directive, one must first understand the theories behind that directive. If the operator (designer) does not possess a sound knowledge of the principles of perspective, the computer will not be able to compensate for that lack of knowledge. Consequently, the computer can be a lightning-fast means to an end only if the designer knows how to get to that end without the aid of the computer in the first place.

Most visual artists, and particularly theatre designers, have had some degree of training in drawing. However in depth the nature of that experience, drawing is still the most common, if not absolute, way of initially expressing one's self. To some designers, drawing is not relegated to that initial expression alone but is also the method of choice to convey the end product of their efforts. Whether rebuffed by the intricacies of building miniature models or confounded by the wizardry of the computer screen, many traditional artisans find pride and fulfillment in the magic created when pencil and brush are put to paper. With personal touches of light and shadow, a nuance of eloquence is created that remains distinctly unlike anything else they may have done. While a model may allow for minute scrutiny, and a computer may offer a paint palette with thousands of colors, a certain type of craftsman will still marvel as each new drawing reveals the phenomenon of perspective in colors that are the result of personal effort and choice and that are only suitable for this one artistic expression.

This book is directed, then, to those individuals who wish to explore a world that may at first appear defined by the parameters of the drawing board, but which is in fact a world of endless dimensions. When a designer elects to portray a design via a rendering, that designer must possess the ability to portray (convincingly) three dimensions while using only two. Learning the tenets of perspective and becoming confident in their use will allow the designer to find solutions to problems of picturization: problems that to the inexperienced may appear to add up to an overwhelming visual puzzle. It is a puzzle, however, in which all of the solutions are literally before one's eyes.

This book will deal specifically with the creation and use of the **perspective grid** as a tool for design presentation. It will endeavor to instruct one on how to convert a scaled floor plan to a presentation-quality rendering. Again, this is not a book on scenic design but rather a guide on *how to render a design*. Although the act of doing a perspective rendering is a part of the creative process of design, it is essential that initial sketches or representative dimensions be provided before work on the grid may begin. It is also important to note that the stage setting is not designed on the perspective grid. The grid is used primarily to ensure accurate placements and spatial configurations of objects as they would appear in perspective. Of course, attitudes of balance and postures of weight when correctly drawn will convey a spatial reality that might require changes in focus or line. Such changes will affect the design to a greater or lesser degree, and therefore, the work done on the grid can become part of the adjustment stage of the creative process. This book's purpose is to instruct one in the use of the **perspective grid** and to expedite drawing procedure. Correctly working on the grid will ensure that the finished rendering will faithfully display the intended stage picture.

To some, the information that follows in the instructional chapters of this book may seem alien, but in fact the visual imageries could not be more commonplace. That which is all around us is often taken for granted. For example, distant objects seem smaller than objects nearer to us. The aisles in the supermarket do seem to diminish in size and move closer together as they retreat from us. Studying perspective pushes one beyond the day-to-day assumptions of visual phenomena and teaches one to observe illusions and investigate why things appear as they do. Of course, to become comfortable with the theories of perspective and confident in one's ability to apply them, practice and patience are essential. Like any other challenge, correct procedure combined with frequency of use will provide visual articulation and furnish enormous artistic satisfaction.

What follows is an invitation to investigate the magic of perspective and explore its wondrous surround.

2. The Perspective Phenomenon

What is **perspective**? Put simply, perspective is an illusion drawn or painted on a two-dimensional surface that attempts to convey an appearance of depth or protrusion. Children learn to achieve basic perspective by drawing a set of railroad tracks that seem to disappear over the horizon. To the adult, this rudimentary representation of perspective pales when compared with modern technical sophistication and computerized wizardry, but to the child, there is delight in such an elementary illustration. The railroad tracks eventually become a set of telephone poles, a pair of picket fences, or a row of buildings that enchants and stimulates the child to expand the drawn horizon and further explore new worlds of picturization.

Prehistoric peoples attempted to capture on cave walls that which they revered and depended upon for their very existence. Some cave paintings showcased solitary creatures, while others integrated human likenesses and relayed in composite form a particular quest or series of events. Using a mixture of coal, crushed chalk, and animal fat combined with the pulp of roots, berries, and earth pigments, early humans (armed with their staple values of red, black, and ochre) labored to duplicate images of the world around them.

Although cave art is commonly classified as "primitive," many of these 20,000-year-old images reflect a power and majesty lacking in the paintings of later, "advanced" peoples. Many of the bold and free strokes seem oddly compassionate and sensitive in nature and allude to a genuine fascination with, and respect for, the animals portrayed. Moreover, because cave paintings are the most abundantly surviving examples of prehistoric artistic expression, we are able to draw some conclusions about early attempts at pictorial representation. It would seem that primitive humans attempted to lend a dimension, or depth, to their picturizations. Cave paintings discovered in France indicate that cave artisans took advantage of curvatures and depressions in rock surfaces to give a three-dimensional appearance to the animals. The desire to portray beings and episodes in highly accurate, duplicative form soon became a necessity as such drawings and paintings began to serve as a record of life's significance. In that capacity, it is thought that the paintings eventually became exalted to the point of worship.

As the need to recount events through visual narratives increased, so did the desire to capture those images in factual and representative detail. However, attention to minute characteristics, pictorial likeness, and "realistic" proportion and spacing did not emerge with any surety until the Greek surge of artistic exploration in the sixth century B.C. The Greeks appear to be the first civilization to seriously concern themselves with spatial proportion and dimensions of depth, and this concern was to extend to complex, three-dimensional sculpture and bas-relief carving. Regardless of the extent of three-dimensional exploration by the Greeks, the development of pictorial perspective (that is, a three-dimensional representation on a two-dimensional surface) was, apparently, a solitary and unrelated curiosity and involved a slow evolutionary process marked by centuries of guesswork. Not until the Italian Renaissance did visual trial and error finally culminate in a more thorough understanding of the mathematics and science of perspective.

One would think that ancient civilizations might have explored the science of pictorial perspective. Architectural achievements prior to Greek advancements are evident in spectacular ruins dotting the Mediterranean and Middle East, as well as evidence gleaned from ancient tablets describing the life and the accomplishments of its peoples. It seems natural, sequentially, that ancient and gifted architects and builders preplanned their projects through sketches and representative likenesses in order to visualize the finished structure. Perhaps such artisans saw no need to attempt to draw their designs and instead built scaled models. After all, the fruits of their efforts would materialize in three-dimensional form. An apparent likeness or simulation of an object was, perhaps, not as important as the tangibility of the real thing, albeit in a reduced scale. Beauty was fleeting, whereas the need for practicality was timeless.

　　　　　　　　　　　　　　The Perspective Phenomenon

Conceivably, the desire to portray (draw and paint) things as they really were was tantamount to duplicating something that already existed. What would be the point of the exercise? If one wished to see a building or a street, why not simply venture outside and see the real thing? It is entirely possible that those objects relegated by previous civilizations to depiction by painting were done so because the scenes expressed figures of legend, worship or general exultation and, therefore, such images might best be rendered in the stately, though unnatural, stature they deserved.

Preclassical Greece

For thousands of years, two-dimensional configuration in painting was standard. The use of only the frontal planes of figures was rampant; depth was only alluded to by overlapping arms, legs, pieces of furniture, and the like, and the effect of foreshortening was nonexistent. Grading color values to suggest distant objects (as in aerial perspective) was light-years away, and any attempts at a proportional diminution of background objects resulted in placing such elements directly above the prominent foreground figure(s).

Building the great pyramids of ancient Egypt was an architectural task unlike any other in the history of the world. Painting a resemblance of the pharaoh to inhabit one of them was an entirely different matter. While heads, arms, legs, and feet were consistently shown in profile, the eyes, chest, and pelvis were always facing front. A change of position was achieved by placing an arm across the chest for a three-quarter appearance, while any suggestions of depth were conveyed by overlapping the legs and feet (fig. 1). There was virtually no foreshortening in any current artistic sense of the word.

The Egyptians were not alone in their stilted depictions of form and setting. The collected magnificence of the Babylonians, the Assyrians, the Minoans of Crete, and the splendor of Mycenae all failed to encourage any changes in the art of picturization. It is remarkable that artisans seemed satisfied for millennia to draw with little more than a slight indication of depth or natural portrayal even those objects which could commonly be seen on a daily basis. However, in light of other significant advancements to the Greek way of life, it is not surprising that the

Figure 1. Egyptian funerary papyrus, XII Dynasty. Reprinted by permission of The Metropolitan Museum of Art, Museum Excavations, Rogers Fund, 1930.

people of Greece, blessed with agile and ever-curious minds, took note of the beauty they saw around them and aspired to portray things as they really appeared. On one such quest for more realistic depiction, the Greeks originated perspective drawing.

Greece and Rome

The Greek pursuit of a refined and lifelike approach to artistic expression was slow but methodical. The earliest evidence of "shadow painting" (*skiagraphia*), where efforts at plane recession would seem to occur, were credited to the ancient scene painter Agatharchus by Vitruvius:

In the first place Agatharchus, in Athens, when Aeschylus was bringing out a tragedy, painted a scene, and left a commentary about it. This led Democritus

The Perspective Phenomenon

and Anaxagorus [both physicists] to write on the same subject, showing how, given a centre in a definite place, the lines should naturally correspond with due regard to the point of sight and the divergence of visual rays, so that by this deception a faithful representation of the appearance of buildings might be given in painted scenery, and so that, though all is drawn on a vertical flat façade, some parts may seem to be withdrawing in to the background, and others to be standing out in front. (Vitruvius 1960, 198)

To the fifth-century Greek, the talent of Agatharchus must have been mystifying. Plutarch, in his *Lives*, relates the story of the great military statesman Alcibiades and his fascination with the paintings of Agatharchus:

[Alcibiades] . . . the force of his eloquence, the grace of his person, his strength of body, joined with his great courage and knowledge in military affairs, prevailed upon the Athenians to endure patiently his excesses . . . as, for example, he kept Agatharchus, the painter, a prisoner till he had painted his whole house, but then dismissed him with a reward. (Plutarch 1909, 22–23)

Vitruvius was to interpret the writings of Agatharchus, Democritus, and Anaxagorus with almost five hundred years of added wisdom, given the advancements in his day of not only the art of painting but also the science of optics. Even as early as the third century B.C., Euclid, in his *Optics*, posed several theorems:

4: When objects are situated along the same straight line at equal intervals, those seen at the farther distance appear smaller.
10: Of planes lying below the eye [level], the farther parts appear higher.
11: Of planes lying above the eye [level], the farther parts appear lower.
12: Of lines which extend forward [toward the observer], those on the right seem to swerve to the left, and those on the left to the right. (Euclid 1886, vol. 6)

Despite the existence of these theorems, the key observations they made did not seem to be applied with any regularity or conviction to the arts. By studying an art comparative to scene painting, particularly that of vase painting, it seems likely that Agatharchus's gift was rudimentary and indicated only the beginnings of perspective illusions as we know them today. What Vitruvius appears to describe, and what will be discussed momentarily, was the fashionable practice of dimensional painting that occurred in homes on the Palatine in the Republic of Rome during the first century B.C.

The Perspective Phenomenon

Elements of perspective that we have come to recognize did not appear overnight. But where the Greeks differed from their predecessors was in their intellectual analysis of everyday things both mundane and beautiful. They were critical *observers*. Greek artists came to realize the now common phenomenon that distant objects appear smaller than nearer objects of the same size. This significant observation of size diminution led to a knowledge of **foreshortening**, whereby objects pointed away from the observers will appear to decrease in size.

"Appear to decrease": Perspective, complete with all its foreshortening, is actually a wonderful trickery of illusion that attempts to duplicate reality. This trickery in painting, which eventually was to incorporate even painted shadows, was scrutinized by Plato in his *Republic*:

You may look at a bed or any other object from straight in front or slantwise or at any angle. Is there then any difference in the bed itself, or does it merely look different? . . . does painting aim at reproducing any actual object as it is, or the appearance of it as it looks? In other words, is it a representation of the truth or of a semblance? (Plato 1941, 328)

Plato continues his analysis of the worth of the painter's illusion during his dialogue on dramatic poetry, stating the appeal of painting to the emotions, but not to reason:

An object seen at a distance does not, of course, look the same size as when it is close at hand; a straight stick looks bent when part of it is under water; and the same thing appears concave or convex to the eye misled by colors. Every sort of confusion like these is to be found in our minds; and it is this weakness in our nature that is exploited, with a quite magical effect, by many tricks of illusion, like scene-painting and conjuring. . . . Paintings . . . are far removed from reality, and that element in our nature which is accessible to art and responds to its advances is equally far from wisdom. (Plato 1941, 334–35)

With this, Plato denounces and dismisses painting as trickery and weakness. It could be argued that such criticism was a factor in the lack of artistic attention given to developing perspective and faithful two-dimensional representations.

Regardless of the impact of Plato's work on the artisan, **linear perspective,** or the appearance of depth whereby objects have receding planes (for example, the railroad tracks), did not advance beyond the level of the individual's ability to acutely observe what was to be painted. As critical observers, Greek artisans could have been more than capable of conceiving a picture or painting that exhibited elements of perspective. What is highly unlikely is that they could have explained why they were doing what they were doing other than to declare that they were drawing or painting what they saw. There is no evidence to suggest that any study or theory of perspective illusion was undertaken. Like the Romans who followed, the power of accurate observation was the primary requisite to artistic accomplishment, but a good eye did not imply an understanding of principles.

Striking perspective illusions can be traced to the first century B.C., as found in wall paintings from the cubiculum of the villa from Boscoreale (Bieber 1961, 124–25). Other spectacular examples were unearthed from Pompeii and obviously predate the eruption of Mt. Vesuvius, ca. 79 A.D. From both locales come astonishing examples illustrating a basic attribute of linear perspective: that a set of parallel lines (for example, the top of a straight roof and the building's bottom, if resting on flat ground), one of which is located below the eye level of the observer and the other of which is located above eye level, will slope toward each other as the object's (building's) side appears to move away from the observer.

Close scrutiny of these paintings will indicate, however, that what does not seem to have been in practice was the principle that parallel lines should converge to a **vanishing point**. And provided the lines drawn are suggesting features that are also parallel with level ground, the vanishing point must occur at the **eye level of the observer**, which according to the phenomenon of perspective is also **the horizon line**. The splendid wall paintings from Boscoreale are full of buildings with colonnades and overhanging balconies, interiors with enormous urns, and pieces of furniture strewn inside and out in a garden setting. One will note, however, that there is more than one **eye level** at work here. Despite its a painted architectural splendor, the wall painting resembles a series of individual studies that appear strangely disjointed and clearly lack evidence of a cultivated knowledge of vanishing-point principles (fig. 2).

Considering the age in which these frescoes were painted, what one sees is quite an extraordinary achievement. But although sets of receding parallel lines are painted as if to eventually converge, they do so in a random appearance. Extending the lines on any given structure will approximate a convergence, but will not occur at one vanishing point. Also, several of the individual buildings are seen from different observation points and eye levels, as if the observer were moving from one

Figure 2. Wall painting from the Cubiculum of the Villa at Boscoreale. Reprinted by permission of The Metropolitan Museum of Art, Rogers Fund, 1903. All rights reserved, The Metropolitan Museum of Art

side to another and climbing a ladder so as to alter the height of the viewpoint. What is lacking is a cohesiveness, a unity of configuration. Each structure in the wall painting would appear to have been viewed, and drawn, separately. What one sees is an interesting collage of impressive three-dimensional structures, each drawn in isolation without any adherence to the principles of linear perspective.

The Perspective Phenomenon

It seems likely that the Roman painters, like their Greek predecessors, were excellent observers who were able to distinguish the many facets of individual structures and relay them in striking detail. But what escaped the ancient artisans was an appraisal of the picture as a whole, for within the larger image many fallacies of perspective composition exist. The keen observer must deduce that both the awareness of, and theory behind, the vanishing-point principle were virtually unknown at that time. Despite the custom that seems to have been common among the wealthy of Rome (and even in fifth-century Greece, according to Plutarch) to decorate their dwellings and their "winter dining rooms" with paintings on grand subjects, the ability to paint these larger scenes convincingly was a random gift and not based on any known perspective theory (Vitruvius 1960, 209).

If the writings of Vitruvius and the theorems professed by Euclid are accurate, and if the Greeks and Romans were acquainted with linear perspective as it was to be systematized during the Italian Renaissance, then it follows to assume that all such knowledge was merely conceived by mathematicians and philosophers and not put into common practice by the artisans. And what is most important to stress is not whether the ancients understood the principles of perspective, vis-à-vis optic theory, but whether those principles were implemented by the art world.

The true paradox is that although the Greeks' curiosity of perspective was inspired by the work of a scene painter, the very nature of the theatre with its numerous spectators and countless lines of sight would seem to have negated any purpose for seriously exploring the perfection of the perspective illusion. From the spectators' standpoint, it would have been virtually impossible for an illusion to have been created that would appear credible from all seats in the theatre. Of course, the same holds true today.

It would not be until the fifteenth century of the Italian Renaissance that linear perspective would be formalized into an established, foolproof, methodical formula. **One-point perspective** (whereby an entire picture or painting appeared to be viewed from one point of observation and all receding lines of a "parallel" structure converged at one vanishing point) became the delight not of an arbitrary group of artisans but of virtually all who were seriously devoted to this wondrous illusion. Ironically, the laws of perspective were developed by the same type of people who, in ancient times, could carry its principles no further: artists. **One-point perspective** has now been developed to such a degree of accuracy and implemented so extensively as to be ingrained; departures from its pictorial theory and improprieties of visual credibility can be spotted by an elementary school child.

The Italian Renaissance

Two men of the early Italian Renaissance given the most credit for the "invention" and advancement of perspective theory were Filippo Brunelleschi (1377–1447) and Leon Battista Alberti (1404–1472). It might be fair to say that Brunelleschi was the first to initiate a serious study of perspective, while Alberti can be recognized for expanding on Brunelleschi's work and synthesizing it into applicable theories of practice.

The changes in size of persons and objects in relation to the position of the viewer, and the seeming convergence of parallel lines over a distance were known, though not with great certainty, at the time Brunelleschi began his study. The move from two-dimensional to three-dimensional painting was largely achieved in the fourteenth century through the paintings of Giotto, and though such an infatuation with the third dimension was short-lived, renewed interest did occur about the time Brunelleschi was beginning his study.

In his research and experimentation conducted in the piazza surrounding the Baptistry of Santa Giovanni in Florence, Brunelleschi could well have perfected the notion of vanishing points. The baptistry is an octagonally shaped structure and the view that Brunelleschi assumed was across the Piazza del Damno and within the middle door of the Cathedral of Santa Maria del Fiore. The cathedral door was (is) situated perpendicular to the center of the baptistry's façade. Brunelleschi, when standing within the doorway to the cathedral, had a perfectly centered view of the baptistry. The cathedral's doorway enclosure would have acted as a sort of framing device that limited his field of vision. Though his field was somewhat large, the concept of a limited area of vision is, of course, not at all dissimilar to the selection of visual images represented on a piece of drawing paper. Either surface upon which the images are realized can be called the **picture plane**.

Staring straight at the baptistry while directly perpendicular to the center of its protruding entrance door meant that the two faces of the octagon on either side of the entrance doors moved away *in actuality*

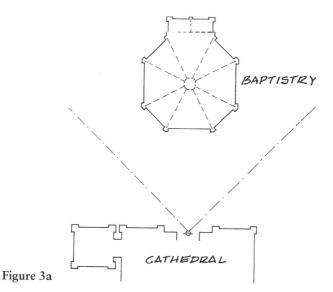

Figure 3a

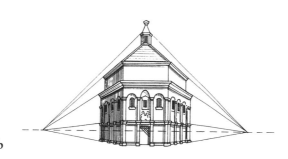

Figure 3b

from Brunelleschi at an angle of 45° (fig. 3a). He was aware of the actual shape of the baptistry. With this knowledge, Brunelleschi observed and conceivably discovered that top and bottom parallel lines representing a surface 45° from the picture plane would result in those two lines converging *at eye level* at a point to the side of his central line of sight. He may also have deduced that, as there were two 45° sides within his view, each one related to a vanishing point equidistant on either side of the central line of sight (fig. 3b). One might also wonder if Brunelleschi made one more vital discovery: *that the distance between a side vanish-*

ing point and the central line of sight as marked along eye level would have been the same distance as from this central point to the spectator, thus arriving at a theory that would later become the **distance point method of perspective**.

To attribute this last discovery to Brunelleschi is conjectural. Even though the preface of Alberti's book *Della Pittura* was dedicated to Brunelleschi, lack of an accurate record by either Brunelleschi or his biographers has led most scholars to conclude that the **distance point method** should be attributed to Alberti because of the highly descriptive analysis found in *Della Pittura*.

Perspective was concerned at the time with the representation of towns, their buildings, and, in particular, the public square. The square was often created first in the drawing, with the town constructed around it. As such, the square was to be a place of architectural proportion and accord, a setting befitting the social man. As Alberti was to note in his book on architecture, there was a need for a public square "where young men may be diverted from the mischievousness and folly natural to their age; and, under handsome porticos, old men may spend the heat of the day, and be mutually serviceable to one another" (Clark 1969, 99). It seemed logical, given the feeling of the day, that the piazza, or square, replete with its order and proportion, might be the most appropriate venue in which to study the theories of perspective. Little wonder that for the many years of perspective paintings to follow, the predominant focus for the artist's work was architectural duplication.

The aspect of perspective theory that perplexed Brunelleschi was not the matter of vanishing points. The fact that they occurred on the horizon line, or at the eye level of the viewer, was a principle that he was able to prove with relatively little difficulty. What Brunelleschi attempted to formulate was a system of measurement. He studied the proportional diminution of equally spaced and sized objects as they retreated from the observer. To lend a simple analogy, once one has drawn a set of railroad tracks in perspective using a central vanishing point, how does one then decide how far apart to space the ties that hold up the track? And how can the spacings between the ties diminish so as to convey a realistic illusion of size diminution? Of course, Brunelleschi did not have railroad tracks to study; if he had, perhaps his task would have been easier. Instead, the tiles, or squares of pavement, in a public square were the models used for his experimentation.

Brunelleschi was not satisfied merely to make a picture look convincing. His goal was to find a legitimate method of illustration that was

The Perspective Phenomenon

not only correct, but one that would impress the viewer as being literal and precise. Whether he achieved his goal is a matter of scholarly debate. However, the writer who was to systematically analyze and record his theories in a published work is not debatable: Leon Battista Alberti, who in his treatise *Della Pittura* (*On Painting*—1435) formulates the distance point method of perspective by means of his *costruzione legittima*, which today is recognizable to artists and draftspersons as the **perspective grid**.

Truly a Renaissance man, Alberti excelled in architecture, painting, playwrighting, poetry, music, mathematics, philosophy, and writing. Following the publication of his *Della Pittura*, anyone wishing to learn to draw correctly was directed to "the mathematicians and Alberti" (Gadol 1969, 21). Alberti believed that the solution to correct picturization could be found in mathematics. What Alberti did was to collate theories of optics and geometry and reduce the essentials to an uncomplicated system; he applied a theory of vision to the art of painting.

Alberti presented a refinement of the ancient and medieval optic theory, which holds that everyone sees in "a cone of vision." Alberti altered the cone to a *piramide visiva*, or **visual pyramid**. The eye is at the top of the pyramid. Looking down through the pyramid to its base, one can see left and right, up and down, and the extent of the field of vision will increase or decrease in size dependent on whether the viewer is looking at something relatively nearby or far away (fig. 4). Alberti likened the painter's canvas to a window that cuts across the visual pyramid. From an established stationary point on this side, the painter looks through the window to the view outside. The painter must then (on the two-dimensional surface of the window or canvas) represent the three-dimensional reality seen beyond.

The reality beyond was to take the form of the "tiles in the public square," and these tiles, or squares in the pavement, when seen in perspective, were to become his *costruzione legittima*, or the legitimate procedure used for the correct spatial placements of objects in perspective. Alberti conducted his observations by using a box closed in on three sides and the bottom. At one end of the box and centered between its vertical corners he made a type of peephole that served, when looked through, as a fixed height for observation. On the floor of the box was placed a painted checkerboard. From the peephole to the corners of the squares of the checkerboard Alberti stretched thin threads; each of the threads attached to a row of the checkerboard (that is, the horizontal rows as seen through the peephole) (fig. 5a). By carefully examining

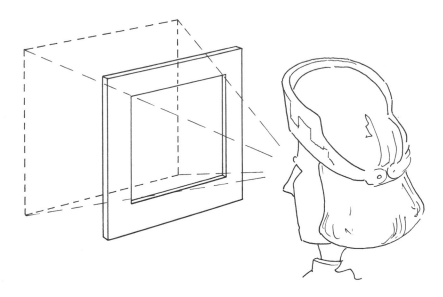

Figure 4

ALBERTI'S VISUAL PYRAMID

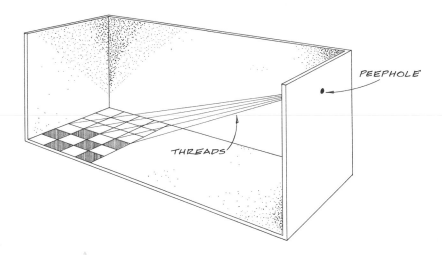

PEEPHOLE

THREADS

Figure 5a

the threads from the side view (from the open side of the box), he was able to place a vertical panel between the peephole and the edge of the checkerboard. Where each thread from the peephole passed the edge of the panel on its way to the checkerboard a mark was made (Ivins 1973, 16–17) (fig. 5b). Through careful study and copious measure-

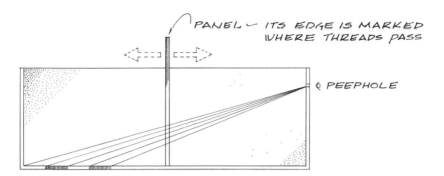

PANEL ~ ITS EDGE IS MARKED
WHERE THREADS PASS

PEEPHOLE

Figure 5b

ments, Alberti transferred his dimensions to a working drawing. He then described how to plot what he observed so as to re-create in perspective the appearance of the checkerboard, or pavement squares:

First of all, on the surface on which I am going to paint, I draw a rectangle of whatever size I want, which I regard as an open window through which the subject to be painted is seen; and I decide how large I wish the human figures in the painting to be. I divide the height of this man into three parts, which will be proportional to the measure commonly called a *braccio* [approx. 2′]; for as may be seen from the relationship of his limbs, three *braccia* [6′] is just about the average height of a man's body. With this measure I divide the bottom line of my rectangle into as many parts as it will hold; as this bottom line of the rectangle is for me proportional to the next transverse equidistant quantity seen on the pavement. Then I establish a point in the rectangle wherever I wish; and [since] it occupies the place where the centric ray strikes, I shall call this the centric point. The suitable position for this centric point is no higher from the base line than the height of the man represented in the painting, for in this way both the viewers and the objects in the painting will seem to be on the same visual plane. [The exact distance of this point from the bottom line would match *identically* the height of the peep hole from the bottom of the box.] Having placed the centric point I draw lines from it to each of the divisions on the base line. These lines show me how successive transverse quantities change to an almost infinite distance. (Alberti 1972, 55) (Fig. 5c)

The terminology used by Alberti is not the same as that which is used today. There was no mention of **vanishing points, orthogonals, station points, observation points,** or the like. When Alberti referred to the "centric point," he was suggesting the **central line of sight** that, when placed at the suggested height of the figure standing on the base line, also corresponds to the eye level of the observer. It is now a well-known

The Perspective Phenomenon

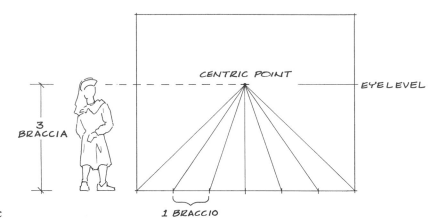

CENTRIC POINT

EYE LEVEL

3 BRACCIA

1 BRACCIO

Figure 5c

phenomenon that the terms **eye level** and **horizon line** are synonomous in perspective nomenclature. The horizon line will always appear at the eye level of the observer; whether one stands full height, climbs a ladder, sits in a chair, or lies on the beach, the horizon line will invariably appear as equal in height to one's eye level. What Alberti was suggesting was that a **central vanishing point** be located in the middle of the picture plane at the eye level of the observer. We now know this as the **horizon line**: "this line . . . as it passes through the centric point . . . may be called the centric [horizon] line" (Alberti 1972, 57).

The panel containing the marks is placed to one side of the drawing. It is arranged so that the lowest mark on the panel is even with the bottom line on the drawing. Horizontal lines are extended (parallel with the centric, or **horizon line**) from each mark so as to cross the lines extending back to the centric point (or **central vanishing point**). These newly drawn horizontal lines indicate the receding horizontal rows of the checkerboard. Alberti was able to check the accuracy of his drawing by scribing a diagonal line through the checkerboard (fig. 6a). If the line passed cleanly from each square's corner to its diagonal corner and in a successive pattern through the entire checkerboard, then the diminution of the horizontal planes of the checkerboard (or **transversals**) was proportionally accurate according to the height of observation and its distance from the image portrayed.

The panel upon which Alberti marked the thread lines acted as a vertical intersection of the visual rays between the peephole, or **observation point**, and the checkerboard. Besides his "window" analogy, this intersection may have been Alberti's most significant contribution. The

The Perspective Phenomenon

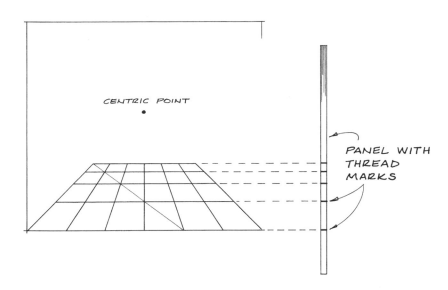

CENTRIC POINT

PANEL WITH
THREAD
MARKS

Figure 6a

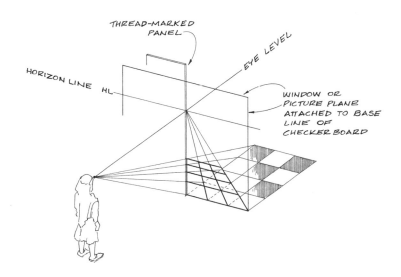

THREAD-MARKED
PANEL

HORIZON LINE   HL

EYE LEVEL

WINDOW OR
PICTURE PLANE
ATTACHED TO BASE
LINE OF
CHECKER BOARD

Figure 6b

intersection refers to a surface upon which all of the images in the background (or that which is seen through the window) are placed. The surface of this window later became known as the **picture plane** (fig. 6b).

It is unclear in the evolution of Alberti's work the point at which the picture plane acquired a fixed position. Through his demonstrations

The Perspective Phenomenon   23

with the "peep show," it seems evident that both the peephole and the checkerboard were in fixed positions. That is, the distance between the two was not variable. At some point, Alberti assigned the picture plane a fixed position by simply attaching the window to the base line of the checkerboard. In this way, the distance between the point of observation and the picture plane would remain constant.

Alberti now continued the work begun by Brunelleschi's study of the baptistry: the geometric theory behind the relationship of the spectator and certain vanishing points. Alberti theorized that an object (or wall whose bottom rests on a level surface and whose top is parallel with its bottom) that is set at an angle of 45° to the picture plane will have a **vanishing point** on the **horizon line**. The distance between that vanishing point and the central vanishing point will be equal to the distance between the picture plane and the point of observation (sometimes referred to as the **O. P.**, or **observation point**).

Using the squares in the pavement, Alberti designed a rather simple exercise based on the shape of an isosceles triangle. He would begin by drawing a base line suggesting proportionately four braccia, or 8′ in length. Above this line and centered between its ends he would place the centric point (central vanishing point) at a height of three braccia (a measurement Alberti had already determined to be the height of the average man at approximately 6′). Through this centric point Alberti would extend the centric line (the horizon line that appears at eye level)

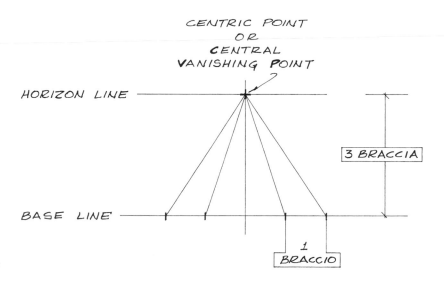

Figure 7

The Perspective Phenomenon

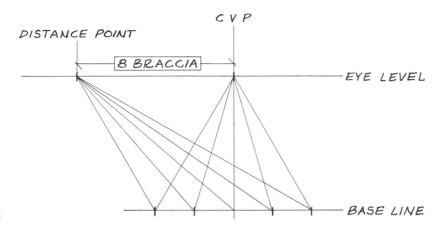

DISTANCE POINT

C V P

8 BRACCIA

EYE LEVEL

BASE LINE

Figure 8

from one end of the picture plane to the other. Proportionate marks of one braccio each would be marked on the base line and from each of these marks a line would be drawn to the centric point (fig. 7).

Alberti would then decide from what distance he wished his squares to appear. Choosing, for example, a distance of four braccia (8′) and based on the theory of the isosceles triangle, he would make a mark on the centric line four braccia to the left of the centric point. This point would be the **distance point**. To the distance point he would connect lines from each braccio mark on the base line (fig. 8). Each of the lines running from the bottom line to the centric point intersected with a line connecting the bottom line with the distance point. Where each intersection occurred indicated the proper placement for the receding horizontal lines (**transversals**) in the pavement. When these transversals were drawn in, the checkerboard arrangement was complete. The check for accuracy using diagonal lines was infallible because the isosceles premise allowed for the use of diagonals to be fundamental to the construction of the checkerboard (fig. 9).

What Alberti achieved was a simple, yet highly accurate system for creating the squares in the pavement. One could draw any size checkerboard provided three essential measurements were known: (1) how many squares were to be shown, (2) the distance from the observation point to the beginning of the picture plane, and (3) the height of observation (specifically the height of the horizon line from the base of the picture plane).

Alberti's distance-point method for perspective was created not so that artists would spend their time drawing checkerboards; rather, its

The Perspective Phenomenon

25

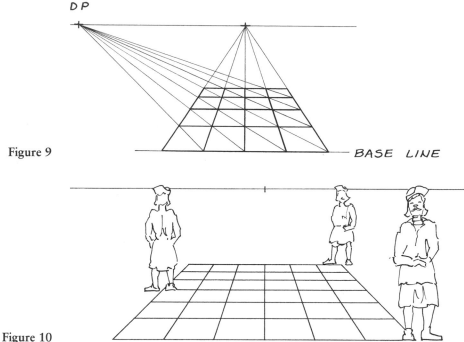

INFALLIBLE ACCURACY

THE DIAGONALS OF ALL FLOOR SQUARES ALIGN WITH THE DISTANCE POINT

DP

Figure 9

BASE LINE

Figure 10

intended purpose was for proportional measuring. The idea was to create a grid for size comparison. The grid was to underlay the drawing, not take precedence over it.

Proportionate sizes could be achieved by drawing a figure of a man in each square along one edge of the checkerboard's receding sides (fig. 10). Because Alberti had initially established his horizon line at approximately 6' high, each of the men's feet would rest on a respective receding square and their head tops would touch the horizon line. In fact, nothing that was over 6' in height would extend over the horizon line. Accordingly, if one of the more distant figures were to appear as if next to an 18' wall, then the height of the man concerned (6') would be tripled to indicate the proportionate height of the structure in perspective. Similarly, a doorway 9' tall would be represented as one and one-half times

The Perspective Phenomenon

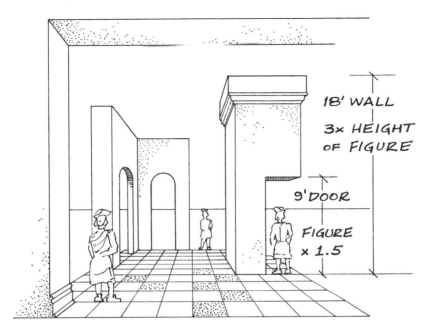

18' WALL

3× HEIGHT OF FIGURE

9' DOOR

FIGURE × 1.5

Figure 11

the height of the figure it framed (fig. 11). The widths of the floor squares were also significant in that they could be used to compare the widths of archways, windows, colonnades, and so on.

Although scholars may dispute the authorship of the perspective formula attributed to Alberti, few could fail to recognize Alberti's efforts to systematize and codify the theories of perspective and geometry into a simple and easily practiced method for painting realistically dimensional scenes. The works of his friends and contemporaries, most notably those of Donatello and Ghibetti, embodied Alberti's perspective formulations. Shortly after the completion of Alberti's *Della Pittura* in 1435, both Donatello and Ghibetti first began to create completely correct perspectival scenes (Gadol 1969, 37n). Somewhat later, in his own treatise on painting, *Trattato*, Leonardo da Vinci mentions Alberti's *Della Pittura* to the extent that he lifted several passages from it and mentions how he studied Alberti's work and improved upon it (Gadol 1969, 12).

Had he been alive, Plato might have been dismayed to see that the one distinct feature of Renaissance painting that set it vastly apart from the collective examples from previous centuries was the desire to truly duplicate appearances. Renaissance painting did not approximate or settle for a "semblance of the truth" but strove even further to "mislead" (in Plato's words) and mystify the onlooker by an attempt at representative duplication. Correct perspectival representation as set forth by Alberti jolted the art world and quickly became the fascination and wonder of almost every painter. Through the centuries, Alberti's methods were practiced by artists of significance such as Serlio, Vermeer, and Canaletto. Countless craftsmen were to implement Alberti's work and many attempted to, and did, refine it.

Perhaps no one from the Egyptians, Greeks, Romans, and medieval artisans down to the early Renaissance and beyond made as vital a contribution to the study and development of artistic perspective as Leon Battista Alberti, who through his lasting marriage of geometry and perspective theories, has been credited with creating the distance point method used to formulate the **perspective grid**.

3. The Perspective Grid: Learning the Basics

The role of the **perspective grid** in theatrical rendering varies from designer to designer. One designer might use it simply as a visual aide to locate approximate positions and sizes of scenic objects, while the other might rely more heavily on it as a precise tool for measuring and placing scenic elements in true perspective. No one should dictate how the grid should be used or under what circumstances. Some designers begin working on a grid so that they may eventually abandon it. They may wish to use the grid merely as a tool for training their eyes and honing their drawing skills so as to ultimately render in a more freehand style. Still others find it an artistic challenge and delight in efforts to master the grid and the representative illusions it affords. Regardless of one's purpose for using the grid, a thorough knowledge of its possibilities can only be an asset to rendering ability and increase one's understanding of perspective.

What the **perspective grid** simulates is, in fact, a bare stage floor. The checkerboard arrangement forms the parameters for both the sections of the stage that will be covered by scenery and the "open" areas necessary for the action of the play, but the multitudes of squares on the grid have virtually no purpose by themselves. The squares are meant to be a comparative aid or, depending on the reason for the grid's use, a measuring tool for transferring the floor plan of the stage setting into a pictorial front view. The finalized floor plan of the setting will be gridded off in the same scale and sized squares as those on the perspective grid. One should be able to look at a square on the gridded floor plan and locate the corresponding square on the perspective grid.

As set down by Alberti, in order to draw a specific perspective grid the following three bits of information are fundamental:

1. *The distance from the observer to the object.* One thing that is a given is that the most advantageous seat for observation is almost always in the very middle of the theatre. Therefore, the line of sight will be centrally located. That, in turn, dictates that the grid is to be constructed around a central vanishing point. The "object" of mention is taken to mean the edge of the perspective grid closest to the observer. Generally, the downstage edge of the grid signifies either the edge of the actual stage or the set line of the stage setting (variations to be discussed later in chapter 5 under "The Thrust Stage" and "The Raked Stage").

2. *The height of the point of observation.* The height of this point is also one's eye level, which, of course, is synonymous with the horizon line. Usually, the best advantage is neither too high nor too low. The height decided upon should show off to the fullest extent the shape of the setting. For instance, a low eye level makes the viewer appear as if he or she were sitting or lying down. As such, too low an eye level placement would result in the bottom of the set appearing flat. The top of the set would be singularly responsible for revealing its complete form. A vantage point from which both the top and the bottom of the set share in the revelation of form is necessary in order for the perspective rendering to be attractive and truly informative.

3. *The size of the object.* This "object" refers to the extent of the physical stage that is needed. One needs to know not only the width of the set and/or playing area, but also the required depth.

Of the above three, only point 3 is a constant: the extent of the needed stage space is something that is determined in early discussions with the play's director well before the rendering is even thought about. Points 1 and 2, however, are determined entirely by the wish of the designer. It might be necessary to illustrate the setting from an extreme distance (for example, the back row), while another designer may wish to show the setting from the front row of the balcony. Each decision is a matter of artistic choice and creative expression.

Before moving on to discuss the drafting tools that are needed to create and work on a perspective grid, one extremely important point needs reiteration:

Very rarely does one design *on* the grid. The act of transferring one's design to the grid generally requires consistent concentration. While some spurts of creativity may occur as the setting takes its proper per-

The Perspective Grid

spective shape, the design itself should have been done in rough form or through rudimentary elevations *before* being transferred to the grid.

The Drafting Tools

Working efficiently on the perspective grid requires precision. Nothing can ensure precision (aside from the concentration of the artist) more than an appropriate **working environment** and **good-quality drafting tools**. Frustrations can be minimized if the working conditions allow attention to be focused on the work and if the tools are reliable.

What should not be minimized is the nature of the working environment. The workspace should be relaxing and free from loud noises and frequent interruptions. Many people find that they need to concentrate on the perspective grid for specific periods of time. Frequent interruptions may make you literally lose your place and have to backtrack. If you like to work to background music, it is suggested that until you become thoroughly familiar with the workings of the grid, the background music be gentle and soothing in nature. Many find they work best if they are not familiar with the music and therefore are not sidetracked by it. Of course, whatever conditions work best for the individual is what is most important.

The tools required for accurately drawing and working on the grid will vary according to individual preference. What should remain standard, however, is that the tools used should be appropriate to the task at hand. Quality drafting tools need not be the most expensive on the market. The tools do not make the artist or draftsperson, but they do make his or her job considerably easier. Following is a list of the basic required tools.

The Drafting Board

The drafting board should be sturdy in construction and can be either a freestanding table or a portable board that sits on a table. Its edges should be perfectly perpendicular and free from any irregularity. Comfortable sizes are 24" x 36" and 30" x 42", though almost any size is suitable. The surface of the board should be covered with a commercially available drafting-board covering, which generally has a slightly cushioned feel and is often a pale green color that minimizes the possibility of eye strain. This covering should never be slit or punctured with compass points, tacks, and so on. Most drafting boards have adjustable settings that allow them to tilt to the desired working angle.

The Horizontal Guide

The horizontal guide may take one of two forms. The first and oldest is the T-square. It is used against the right and left edges of the drafting board for drawing horizontal lines. The most favored type of T-square is made of wood with clear plastic inserts running along both edges of the T's vertical side. The plastic not only allows for the smooth running of pen or pencil along its edge but also allows the artist to see any relative reference points that may be located below the line to be drawn. The length of the T-square should normally be a bit longer than the width of the drawing board so as to allow for the maximum length of line to be drawn on the drafting surface. The main drawback of the T-square is alignment: when drawing perfectly horizontal lines one must consistently check to see that the square is pressed snugly up against the edge of the drafting board. The second type of horizontal guide available is the parallel edge, commercially available under the names *Paradraft* or *Mayline*. This apparatus attaches to the surface of the drafting board by a cable system and runs smoothly up and down while maintaining a perfectly horizontal, or parallel, position. This system is considerably more convenient and reliable than the T-square, but it is also more expensive. It is, however, quite easy to install (fig. 12). (Even if one does use a parallel edge, it is worth holding on to the T-square for drawing long, angled lines and aligning with vanishing points.)

Triangles

Triangles are made of clear plastic and are used for drawing vertical lines in association with the horizontal guide and any other straight lines deviating from horizontal. Triangles come in standard 45° and $3\%0$° shapes and in varying sizes. A large 45° triangle is useful for drawing long lines and a 9" $3\%0$° is helpful (fig. 13). Many triangles feature a step-down edging for inking with technical pens.

The Perspective Grid

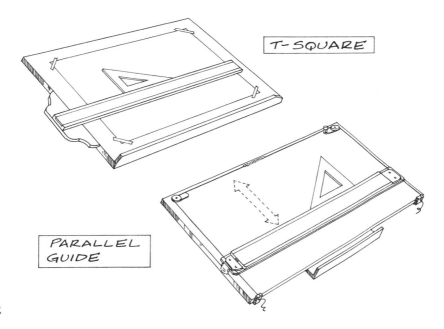

HORIZONTAL GUIDES

T-SQUARE

PARALLEL GUIDE

Figure 12

Scale Rules

Scale rules are available in triangular and flat styles, as well as metric and imperial conversions. The imperial rule is the common one for theatrical use, since theatre in the North American continent measures in terms of feet and inches. The 12" triangular rule that features scales ranging from ⅛" to 3" is the conventional one preferred by most designers (fig. 14).

Templates

Templates come in a wide variety of shapes and sizes. For work on the perspective grid, one should be equipped with two circle templates: a small one (circles ¹⁄₁₆" to 1½") and a large one (circles 1½" to 3½"). It is also good to have ellipse templates featuring varying sizes and degrees and a set of french curves for drawing large curved segments (fig. 15).

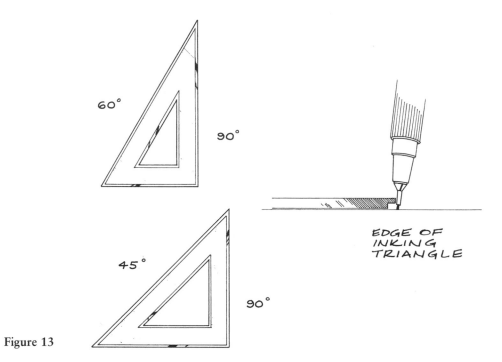

60°

90°

45°

90°

EDGE OF
INKING
TRIANGLE

Figure 13

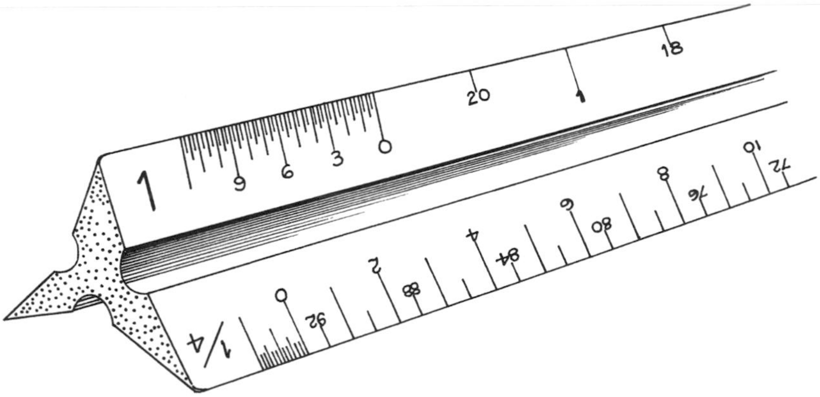

Figure 14

The Perspective Grid

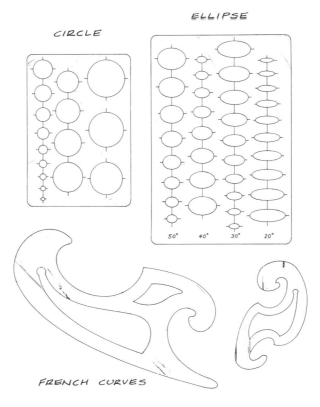

Figure 15

Pencils

Pencils are either wooden or mechanical. Wood pencils will need frequent sharpening (depending on the hardness) and generally are inferior to mechanical ones. Mechanical pencils, like their wood counterparts, are available in a wide range of lead (graphite, actually) hardness. The mechanical pencil can house several thin pieces of lead that are "clicker-advanced" as needed. Distinct from this type is the lead holder, which will hold a single but fatter piece of lead that is sharpened with a lead pointer. The degree of hardness recommended for the perspective grid is the 0.5mm 2H. When used with the mechanical pencil, this lead stays sharp and emits clean, thin lines that are also easily erased. When pencil-shading on the rendering, a variety of softer wood pencils ranging from HB to 4B is recommended (fig. 16a).

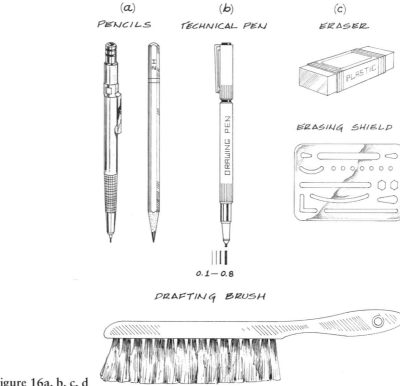

(a) PENCILS   (b) TECHNICAL PEN   (c) ERASER

DRAWING PEN

0.1 — 0.8

ERASING SHIELD

DRAFTING BRUSH

Figure 16a, b, c, d

Technical Pens

Technical pens are handy to use for renderings that require a hard outline to underline watercolor washes. Expensive "rapidograph" pens are not necessary and are inconvenient when the points, or nibs, become clogged with dried ink. What is readily available on the market are disposable pens varying in nib size from 0.1mm to 0.8mm. These come with either a nonpermanent watercolor ink or indelible pigments. The lines flow smoothly, dry quickly, and rarely blot except on a very porous surface. They will not dry out unless left uncapped. Some brands also feature various ink colors. With proper care, these pens will last through several renderings and are quite inexpensive (fig. 16b).

Erasers

Erasers are a matter of personal preference. Avoid hard erasers as they may damage the drawing surface, and too soft erasers that create more mess than efficiency. Erasers are available in block, plug, and pencil form (fig. 16c).

Drafting Brush

A drafting brush is indispensable for removing graphite dust, pencil shavings, or eraser refuse from the drawing surface (fig. 16d).

Illumination

Painters love the daylight, but designers need a consistently strong light source. Any number of drafting board lights and gooseneck lamps are available. A shaded light on a movable apparatus is important so as to avoid glare. Many find fluorescent lights harsh, and opt for a softer incandescent source (fig. 17).

The Drawing/Painting Surface

The drawing/painting surface is dependent on the method of colorization. If one is to perform pencil shading, 16 lb. bond paper is more than suitable, provided there have not been too many erasures. The more erasures, the greater the wearing down of the paper surface and overall thickness; too many erasures will cause shading or coloring media to react in nonstandard ways. What is recommended for a presentation-quality rendering that will stand the test of time is mat board. Mat board comes in an extensive variety of colors and shades. It is durable, will not react unfavorably to normal erasing, and will resist warping when treated with watercolor washes. Avoid using mat board with a textured surface. Choose the smoothest surface type available to avoid line irregularities. Also, if working on a colored mat board, choose a light shade in order to see all of the pencil lines.

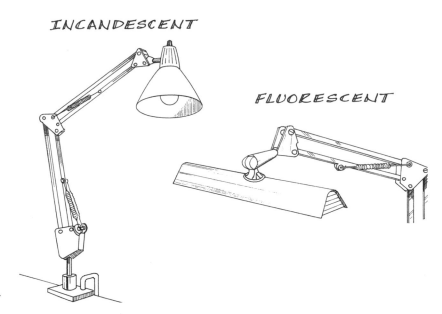

INCANDESCENT

FLUORESCENT

Figure 17

Drafting Tape

Drafting tape resembles masking tape, though it is not as sticky. Drafting tape is more than strong enough to anchor either paper or mat board to the drafting board. Masking tape can often leave a sticky residue, which drafting tape will not. A convenient size is the ¾" wide roll.

As the saying goes, "You get what you pay for." Where drafting equipment is concerned, high-quality products can be bought for a very reasonable price. Proper care of the equipment is essential and will result in long life.

Drawing the Perspective Grid

Having determined the size of the stage space, the height of the horizon line, and the distance from the observation point to the stage, one additional task must be performed before drawing the perspective grid: the floor plan to be transferred must be overlaid with its own grid.

Although the accompanying floor plan will not appear in any of the exercises, it is important to illustrate the manner in which a floor plan

The Perspective Grid

is correctly gridded out. The floor plan is always gridded *after* it has been designed and finalized. To conceive a floor plan on a pregridded sheet is an impediment to creativity and may consciously or subconsciously force the designer into convenient graphic solutions based on the existing grid pattern. Perhaps the best way to grid a floor plan is to mark on a copy of the original floor plan. A **blueline copy**, or what used to be known in its negative form as a **blueprint**, works best. As the name suggests, the blueline is a copy with an off-white background and blue lines notating all of the specifics of the theatre and the stage setting. The photographic process used to create the blueline copy is amazingly accurate in its transfer of scale. A photocopy made on a standard office copier is unreliable when a detailed scale reproduction is needed.

Grid the blueline at the drafting board. (Using red ink or colored pencil for the grid lines nicely distinguishes them from the other elements appearing as blue.) The most common scale used for theatrical floor plans is ½" = 1'–0", and, appropriately, the same scale will be used for the perspective rendering. When transferring the floor plan of a box set, the bottom grid line should occur at the set line. Continue measuring up from this line along the center line in 2' intervals. The last mark made should be upstage of any element of the set that will be seen by the audience. Strike in the horizontal lines wherever there is a mark on the center line and extend the ends of the lines well past the side extremities of the set. Next, draw the vertical grid lines on the floor plan. Along the bottom horizontal grid line (the **set line**, or **S.L.**), measure out from the **center line** (**C.L.**) to the right and left in 2' intervals and mark accordingly. As the center line on the floor plan will also be the center line on the perspective grid, measuring out equally on both sides from the floor plan's center line is essential. Extend the 2' markings out to a point just beyond the sightline extremities. Strike in the vertical lines (fig. 18). It is now time to draw the perspective grid.

NOTE: The following perspective grid is not related to any specific stage setting but rather will conform to the elements that will later appear as instructional illustrations for the use of the perspective grid.

For the sake of clarity, the dimensions for this perspective grid cover a stage area that is 16' wide by 10' deep. The scale is ½" = 1'–0" and the squares represent 2' by 2'. As the method used for drawing the grid is based on Alberti's distance-point method, allow for the placement of the distance point to occur on the drafting board. Then, using a right-handed orientation, align and securely tape down the drawing paper on

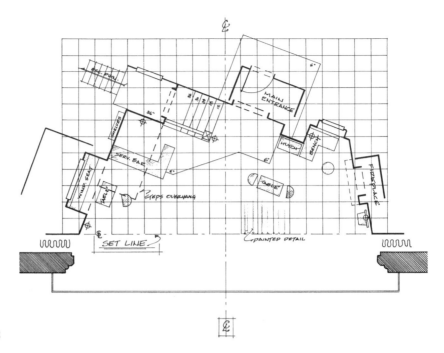

Figure 18

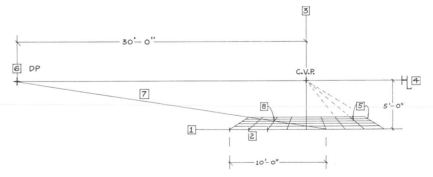

Figure 19

the right side of the drafting board. Proceed with the following steps (fig. 19):

1. Strike a long horizontal line a few inches up from the bottom of the paper. This **base line**, like Alberti's initial line, will refer to the edge of the grid closest to the observation point. Henceforth, this base line shall be referred to as the **first transversal**.

2. Mark off enough 2′ intervals to total the required stage width of 16′. The center mark at the 8′ point will serve not only as the center line of the stage and grid but also as the placement of the central line of sight.

3. From the center mark, draw a vertical line up the height of the paper. Next, the eye level, or **horizon line (HL)** is drawn. What seems to be an ideal height is 5′. Consequently,

4. Measure up from the **first tranversal** along the center line to the 5′ mark and make a small dot on the center line. Through this dot draw a long horizontal line that extends off the paper, onto the surface of the drafting board and to its outer edges. Where the horizon line and the center line intersect will be the **central vanishing point (c.v.p.)** for the perspective grid.

5. From the 2′ intervals on the **first transversal**, draw lines back toward the **c.v.p.** These lines are called **orthogonals**. It is important that they are aligned with the **c.v.p.** without extending all the way to it.

6. Mark the **distance point (DP)**. What seems a favorable distance from which to view a setting is, depending on the nature of the set and the shape of the theatre, 40′. Generally, from this distance one can appreciate the setting without relying on peripheral vision. To conserve space for this illustration the **DP** is set at 30′. Based on right-handed orientation, measure out to the *left* from the **c.v.p.** a distance of 30′ and make a mark.

It is more accurate to signify an important location with a small slash, or hash mark, across the original line rather than making a dot. The intersection of the original line with the hash mark provides a better target for future reference and alignment than a round spot or dot.

Now comes a slight variation to the method described by Alberti. What he did not elaborate on was the determination of the overall depth for his checkerboard arrangement.

7. As the depth for this particular stage is 10′, count from the *left* end of the **first transversal** until the 10′ orthogonal is reached. From this point, align a long straight edge with the **distance point (DP)**. Strike a line from the 10′ **orthogonal** to just past the

Learning the Basics

orthogonal that was drawn from the left end of the **first trans-versal** to the **c.v.p.**

If the *depth of a stage* (or the playing area as designated by the set) *is greather than its width,* extend the FIRST TRANSVERSAL to the right until the desired depth distance has been reached and align this point with the DP.

8. Wherever the line to the **DP** intersects with an **orthogonal**, that point indicates the position of a receding horizontal grid line, or **transversal**. At each intersection, draw a horizontal line extending a little way beyond the far right and far left **orthogonals**.

According to the assigned specifics, the perspective grid is complete. Assuming supporting sketches of the setting have been made, the transfer of the design may begin.

The Basics of Measuring on the Perspective Grid

It is impossible to measure in perspective. Alberti's original checker-board concept did allow for approximating the height of an object based on the representative figure of a 6' (or three braccia) tall man. It is still possible to do such an approximation, but taking a rule, and attempting to measure anything that is upstage of the first transversal of the grid is a futile endeavor. Some perspective grids are drawn with two side grids and a top grid. Though these additional grids will help greatly in the approximation of heights and spatial relationships, they may tend to get in the way and contribute more to visual clutter than efficacious usage.

There is only one place on the grid where scaled measurements can be taken: the **first transversal**. One can measure left, right, straight up, and straight down from it. All measurements must be taken off some part of this line and then, using the central vanishing point or another reference point, the measurements can be projected back (or upstage) to a specific point on the grid.

In order to begin explaining how measuring is done, we must refer to a simple floor plan. Figure 20a shows the stage floor gridded (on ½"

The Perspective Grid

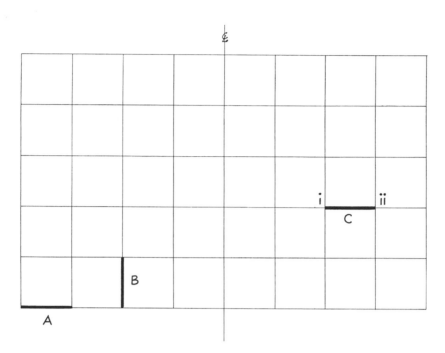

Figure 20a

scale) into 2' squares. Note that the grid lines are of the lightest possible weight so as not to interfere with the notations for all other scenic elements. Again, the grid lines exist solely as the spatial references needed to transfer the floor plan to the perspective grid. They are unrelated to the understanding of the workings of the floor plan and are therefore kept as unobtrusive as possible. (As there are many symbols common to floor plan notation, respective notations will be explained as the need arises.)

The heavier-weighted line marked **A** indicates an element of scenery resting on the floor. This line should be taken to refer to a wall (a stage flat) or some other two-dimensional structure. (A floor plan can furnish much information but cannot answer all questions. A floor plan does *not* provide particulars of the front elevation, for example, heights of walls or the nature of surface treatments, moldings, and so on.) Flat **A** is conveniently resting on the downstage extremity of the floor plan grid, which corresponds to the first transversal on the perspective grid. As flat **A** spans from only one orthogonal to one other, its length is 2'. Finding the corresponding area for its location on the perspective grid is simply

Learning the Basics   43

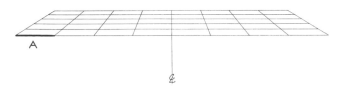

Figure 20b

a visual transfer (fig. 20b). Drawing this line on the perspective grid demonstrates the most basic tenet of the transfer process:

The floor plan positioning of scenic units on the perspective grid must occur before the heights of those units are determined.

As obvious as this tenet may seem, one does not always remember to *work from the ground up*. Even units suspended above the stage floor must be projected first on the perspective grid floor and then raised up as if to appear to be floating.

Now that the base of flat **A** has been drawn on the grid, its height needs to be established. From each end of the flat, vertical lines are lightly drawn to extend generously above the horizon line. Because this flat rests on the first transversal it may be measured directly. The flat is to be 10′ in height, so the measurement is marked on one of the flat's vertical ends and from this mark a horizontal line is drawn connecting the top corners (fig. 20c). (Since it is parallel to the picture plane, the flat will be drawn as a rectangle and will not be foreshortened.) If other units are to be transferred to the grid, it would be premature to darken, or **verify**, flat **A** at this time. Other units might overlap it, or front elevation particulars might be added later.

Flat **B** (fig. 20a) is perpendicular to **A** and rests conveniently on a floor plan orthogonal grid line; it spans from one transversal to one other, *and* one of its ends touches the first transversal. Once again the base of this flat runs 2′ and may be transferred visually without measuring anything. Vertical lines are extended up from the ends of its base. The end of the flat resting on the first transversal may be measured to 10′ and marked. To draw the top edge of the flat, the mark is aligned with the **central vanishing point** and a line is struck to the flat's upstage

The Perspective Grid

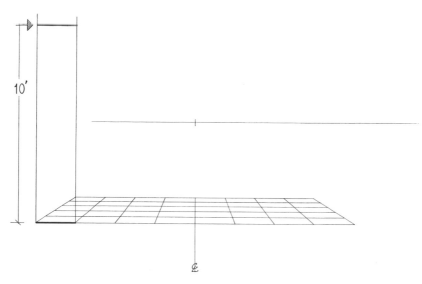

10′

℄

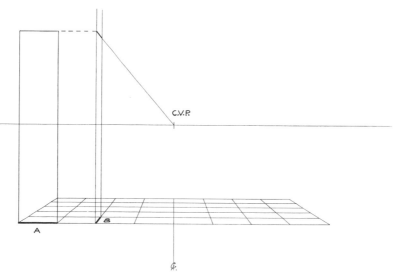

C.V.P.

A   B

℄

top corner (fig. 20d). This action reinforces another fundamental principle:

Any line traveling directly up and downstage, that is, parallel to an orthogonal, will use the central vanishing point of the perspective grid as its vanishing point.

Learning the Basics

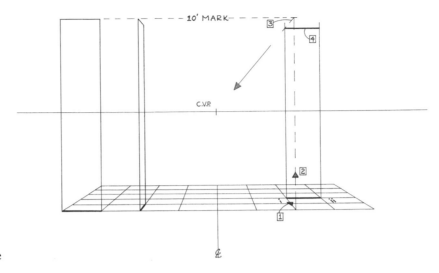

Figure 20e

Flat **C** (fig. 20a), like flat **A**, rests parallel to the observer, but its position is slightly different in that it rests upstage on the third transversal. For simplicity of illustration, its length has been cut off at the intersections of orthogonals and transversals. The base of the flat is located and drawn on the perspective grid, and its vertical ends are struck. Measure this flat to appear in perspective (fig. 20e):

1. With a triangle, align bottom corner **i** with the **c.v.p.** and extend the straightedge downstage to where it crosses over the first transversal and make a mark.
2. From this mark, draw a very light vertical straight up and measure up along this line from the first transversal to the height of 10′ and make another mark.
3. Align this second mark with the **c.v.p.**, and where the straightedge crosses the left-hand edge of flat **C** make a third mark. This mark will indicate a 10′ high flat placed 2′ upstage from the edge of the grid.
4. Draw the top edge of the flat with a horizontal line from the third mark to the right vertical edge of the flat.

The procedure outlined above in steps 1 through 4 is really quite simple: "pull down, measure up, push back." Any line that occurs upstage of the first transversal must be pulled downstage to a reference point on

The Perspective Grid

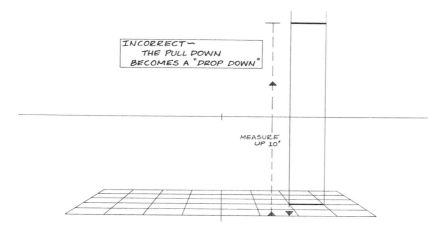

Figure 21

the first transversal where it can be measured vertically to scale and then carried back to the line's point of origin. (Later demonstrations will reveal short cuts to cut down on the amount of measuring. For now, in order to clearly explain measuring procedure, each flat is treated as an isolated unit.)

Both the "pull down" (downstage) and the "push back" (upstage) always refer to alignment with the **c.v.p.** All too often the "pull down" will take the form illustrated in figure 21; the mistake made is really a "drop down" and does not adhere to the perspective grid's orthogonals that are created by alignment with the **c.v.p.**

The three remaining measuring examples in this section pose slightly different challenges in that they involve vanishing points other than the grid's **c.v.p.** Locating and using vanishing points for scenic units will not only ensure correct drawing procedure but will also greatly expedite the drawing process.

Flat **D** (fig. 22a) rests diagonally within one square. Its base can be drawn on the grid by comparison to its position on the gridded floor plan. Locating its vanishing point on the horizon line has already been done. Because it is resting diagonally in a square, its vanishing point will be the same as the **distance point** used to create the receding transversals of the perspective grid (fig. 22b). In a situation like this where it is possible to locate a vanishing point, only one height measurement need be found. Generally, it is easiest to use the bottom corner of the

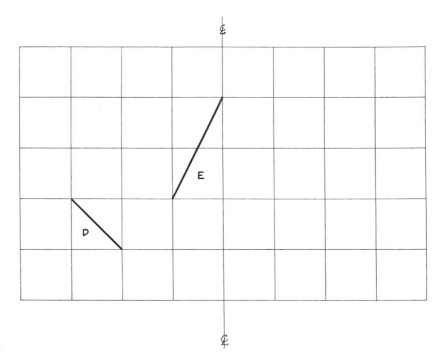

Figure 22a

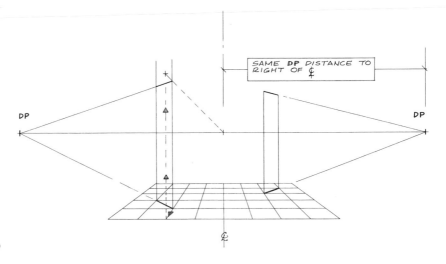

SAME DP DISTANCE TO
RIGHT OF ₵

Figure 22b

The Perspective Grid

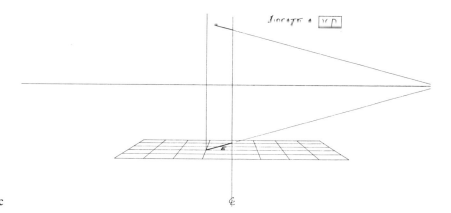

Figure 22c

flat closest to the first transversal. After the "pull down, measure up, and push back mark" has been located, simply align it with the vanishing point (again, in this case, the **distance point**) and draw a line from the mark on the flat's downstage edge to the upstage vertical edge of the flat. To find the vanishing point for a flat sloping diagonally through a floor square to the observer's right (that is, stage left), measure out to the right of the **c.v.p.** the distance of the **DP** and make a mark to signify the flat's **vanishing point.**

Finding the vanishing point for flat **E** is easily accomplished by extending its bottom edge to the horizon line.

To locate a vanishing point, align a straight edge with the bottom of the flat as drawn on the perspective grid. Extend this line to the horizon line and where the two intersect is the vanishing point for that flat.

The completion of the flat's height is achieved in the same manner as flat **D** (fig. 22c). Always check to see if a vanishing point can be found on either the drawing surface or the top of the entire drafting board. It will not harm the surface of the drafting board to lightly extend on to it the perspective grid's horizon line. It is seldom that many of the scenic units' vanishing points will be located on the drawing surface (that is, paper or mat board), but many may be found on the larger expanse of the drafting board.

Some units, however (such as flat **F** shown in fig. 23), will be placed at an angle so slight from a transversal that its foreshortening is gradual to such an the extent that the vanishing point may be located several feet off the drafting board surface. In this case, attempting to locate a

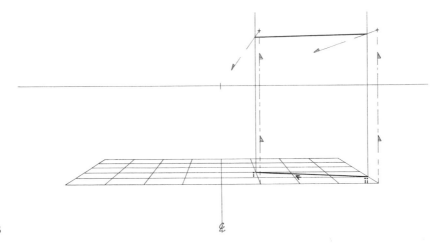

Figure 23

vanishing point is ludicrous. Instead, it will be necessary to "pull down, measure up, and push back" each bottom corner (**i** and **ii**). When the two heights are ascertained, the marks on each vertical side of **F** are joined with a straight line to complete the top edge of the flat.

It is not uncommon to wind up with a completed perspective rendering that has more vanishing points than one can easily count. Stage settings that *realistically* depict interior spaces may have floor plans that make use, predominately, of 90° wall joinery. Figure 24 indicates the three primary arrangements (within which there are countless variations) of realistic interior setting floor plans for the proscenium stage. Example 1 features an expanse of back wall that is parallel to the observer. It is rather static and suggests overall a **symmetrical** approach which, as seen from this view at least, does not seem to invoke much visual interest. The back wall, however, does not pose many pitfalls for perspective drawing. Note that, because of the sightline considerations of audience members seated to the right and left extremes, the two main wall structures coming D.R. and D.L. fail to meet the back wall at 90°. Not only might this arrangement slightly undermine the realistic intent of the setting, but it also implies a very formalized and structured viewing relationship to the audience. Accordingly, the need to "open out" furniture to the audience further subverts the realistic intent as most furniture in dwellings is placed either parallel or perpendicular to wall configurations.

Floor plan examples 2 and 3 are **asymmetrical** in design. That is, what occurs scenically on one side of the center line is markedly differ-

The Perspective Grid

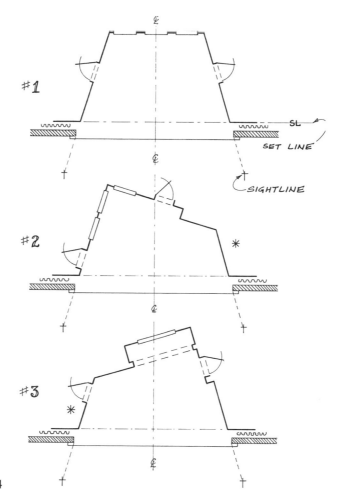

Figure 24

ent from that occurring on the other side. The view the audience receives compared with example 1 is slanted, and, subconsciously, might be justifiably so for dramatic reasons. Regardless, there is considerably more visual interest in 2 and 3 and the preponderance of 90° wall joinery and furniture placements lends realistic credibility. Deciding which of the basic shapes of examples 2 or 3 to use for the design often depends largely on requirements in the play script, such as the number of entrances/exits, dramatic centers of interest, important furniture or scenic units, significant stage business, or whatever. The short walls (*) in examples 2 and 3 have been adjusted to a greater-than-90° joinery to the

Learning the Basics 51

remainder of the set for sightline considerations. Clearly, one may see that when transferring either of these floor plans to the perspective grid, locating vanishing points for as many of the walls that incorporate 90° configurations will greatly expedite the transfer and drawing process. Therefore, locate vanishing points wherever possible!

The Perspective Grid

4. The Perspective Grid: Expanding the Basics

Drawing a perspective rendering of one flat (wall) is really no different from drawing a series of adjoining walls so as to form a basic setting. The setting appears more complex because it is a compilation of many parts. If you can remember to treat each wall or scenic unit on an individual basis, the complexity of the total arrangement will take care of itself.

This section is devoted to the transfer of a simple realistic interior setting to the perspective grid. It not only deals with the placements of the set walls but also explains how to plot door and window openings, portray wall thicknesses (such as in archways), draw the details of door and window units, and add architectural moldings and trim.

As mentioned earlier, the floor plan is designed first and gridded later. The designer rarely knows until the plan is gridded where scenic units will be placed in relation to the grid lines. More often than not, the ends of walls will not conveniently fall on the intersections of orthogonals and transversals, thereby necessitating a means of locating points on the perspective grid other than by way of a handy visual transfer.

In order to be prepared to face the inevitability of "within-square placements" that are apt to occur with even the simplest of floor plan transfers, notice the position of flat **A** in figure 25a. One of its ends (**i**) rests on an intersection and the other (**ii**) does not. The intersection location is transferred visually and marked with a small **dot** on the perspective grid. The other end may be found by way of **line elongation**:

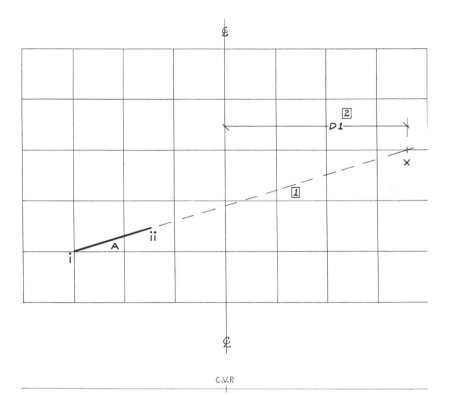

Figure 25a

Figure 25b

1. On the gridded floor plan, align flat **A** with a straightedge, and with a light line extend the base of the flat until it crosses another transversal, and make a mark (**x**).
2. Measure the distance from this mark to the center line of the floor plan (**D1**).
3. Moving to the perspective grid (fig. 25b): On the **first transver-**

The Perspective Grid

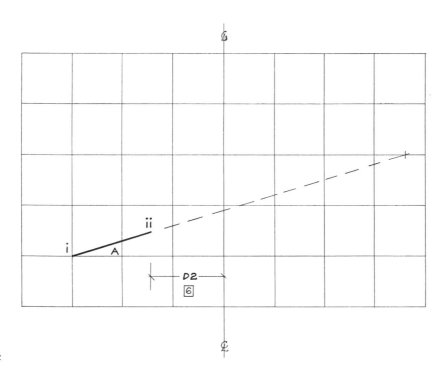

sal, measure out from the center line to the right the distance of **D1** on the floor plan and make a mark (**x**).

4. Align the mark found in number 3, above, with the grid's **c.v.p.** Where the straightedge crosses the upstage transversal corresponding to the one on the floor plan, make a second mark (**x1**).

5. Connect this second mark with a light line to the other end of the wall (**i**), which was **dotted** as occurring at the transversal/orthogonal intersection.

At this point, what has been drawn is the correct positioning of flat **A,** but obviously to a much wider, or longer, dimension than the actual flat drawn on the floor plan (**ii**). Now, the length of the wall on the grid must be established so to represent its intended visual space:

6. On the floor plan (fig. 25c), measure the distance between the end of flat **A** (**ii**) and the center line (**D2**).

Expanding the Basics 55

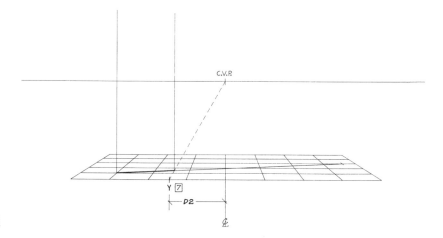

Figure 25d

7. Take the distance found in number 6, and on the perspective grid (fig. 25d) locate the corresponding placement on the **first transversal** and make a mark (**Y**).

8. Align the mark found in number 7 with the grid's **c.v.p.**, and where the straightedge crosses the line elongation of flat **A**, make a mark. This last mark indicates the other end of the set wall (**ii**).

Extend vertical lines up from the ends of flat **A**. Check to see if a vanishing point can be located. If not, it will be necessary to find the heights of both ends of flat **A** individually.

One will develop individual ways of working on the perspective grid and most likely assign personal symbols to particular lines in order to organize and expedite the measuring process. Consequently, it might behoove the designer to label the transversals and orthogonals on the grid and floor plan with numbers and/or letters, for example, T1, T2, O1, O2, and so on, so as not to confuse reference points. Short of this, one should get into the habit of counting squares. For example, note that a point is "up four." Then, when pushing a point back toward the c.v.p., one can count the transversals as they are passed over rather than relying merely on a visual comparison of representative placement.

Line elongation is perhaps the single most important way of locating the majority of points on the perspective grid. Flat **B** in figure 26 looks more challenging to locate on a grid than **A**, above. Perhaps it is, but

The Perspective Grid

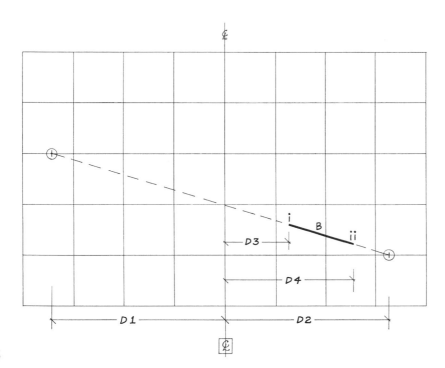

Figure 26

only slightly. Because neither of **B**'s ends falls on an intersection should not cause concern. It simply means that both ends of **B** must be found the same way that the end of **A** (**ii**) was found: on the floor plan elongate the line of the bottom of the flat to cross transversals, measure the mark on the floor plan transversal out from the center line, transfer the measurement to the first transversal of the perspective grid, and push the point back to the **c.v.p.** to determine the elongated ends of the flat. Remember that both line elongations and measuring must take place on the floor plan *and* the perspective grid.

Occasionally, transferring the placement of a flat to the grid is far easier than it looks. In fact, looking carefully is the key. After a while, one will not see just an arrangement of lines to be transferred, but will instead be able to quickly recognize a flat's position and ascertain if some measuring steps can be eliminated. Take, for example, flat **A** as seen in figure 27. Note the end marked **i**. As it turns out, when the floor plan grid was drawn, **i** landed in the very middle of a square. To locate the center of a square on the perspective grid requires no measuring whatsoever. Simply locate the representative square and draw diagonals

Expanding the Basics   57

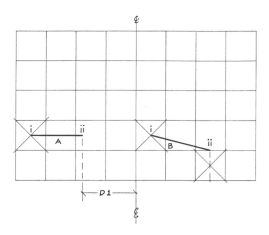

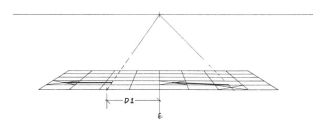

Figure 27

from corner to corner, thus forming an "x" and **subdividing** the square. The intersection of the "x" is the very middle of the square and is, in this case, the location of **i**. Flat **A** rests parallel to two transversals, so drawing it on the grid is simply a horizontal line to the artist's right. Extend the **ii** end a little further than needed, because a quick measurement will be necessary to plot it. Measure the position of **ii** from the floor plan's center line, transfer this distance to the first transversal of the perspective grid, make a mark and push this mark back to the grid's **c.v.p.** Where the "push back" line crosses the elongated line of flat **A** is the **ii** end.

Flat **B** in figure 27 is somewhat easier to plot than **A**. Locating and transferring **i** of **B** is no different than **i** of **A**. Flat **B**'s (**ii**) end is also midway through a square in that it is located on a transversal and in the middle of two orthogonals. This point can be found in one of two ways:

The Perspective Grid

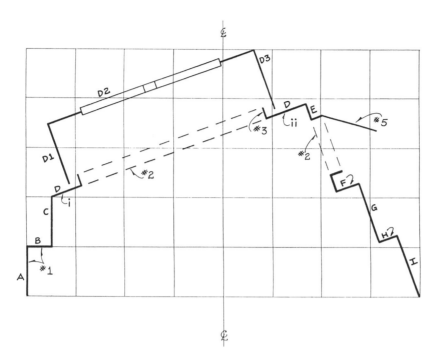

Figure 28a

by measuring out from the center line and pushing back to the respective transversal; or by "X-ing" the square either upstage or downstage of **ii** and, through alignment with the **c.v.p.**, either "pulling down" or "pushing back" to the appropriate transversal and thus finding the position of **ii**.

Transferring a Simple Interior Setting

In order to transfer the floor plan shown in figure 28a to the perspective grid, an explanation of the various line notations on the floor plan is necessary. For clarity, the notations are labeled numerically, while the flats have been assigned letters.

1. A wall resting on the stage floor.
2. An element of scenery suspended above the stage floor. In this case the dash line refers to the top (**header**) of an archway and door opening.
3. A **reveal,** or that which gives the impression of thickness.

Expanding the Basics

4. A window.
5. The actual working door (**shutter**). The position of the door as drawn indicates the manner in which it opens. For simplicity's sake, it will be drawn in its closed position.

NOTE: The following information is rarely provided on a floor plan but is commonly indicated on an accompanying sketch or list of specifics:

- Heights of walls
- Heights of archway, door, and window openings
- Distance from the stage floor to the bottom of the window
- Any indications of architectural trim (for example, moldings) or door and window motifs

All of this omitted relevant information will be provided as the illustration progresses.

Though a fair amount of measuring will come into play in this transfer, once the correct perspective "shell" of the set has been drawn, much of the detail work will be achieved through visual comparison and approximation.

It must once again be stressed that it is best to locate the entire floor plan on the perspective grid before concerning oneself with heights or particulars of the front elevation. In order to clearly illustrate the steps involved in the entire transfer process, some of the following drawings involve variances in the height of horizon lines from the first transversal as well as changes in the distance point measurement. Such changes have resulted in a better viewing of the floor squares on the perspective grid; all drawings have been conceived to scale and no other liberties in their picturization have been taken.

As is common with most theatrical floor plans, individual flats and combinations of flats joined to create long walls have been coded for easy reference to the working drawings. Any manner of coding is appropriate, provided that it is easily understandable and consistent. In some cases, the coding will refer to stock scenic units that are pulled and integrated with other pieces of the setting. Many designers prefer to use a lettering code for flats with numerals for subcoding, such as B1,

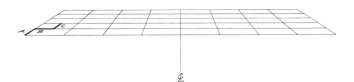

Figure 28b

B2, and so on. For this transfer, the flats have been letter-coded. This floor plan is relatively easy to transfer to the perspective grid, as it is intended to suggest a realistic-style setting that makes use of several 90° corners.

Remembering that *flats with parallel planes* (that is, parallel with one another) *will share the same vanishing point*, one may discern by the angle of many of the wall sections that a vanishing point might be found on either the drawing surface or the drafting board. Flats **D1**, **D3**, **E**, **G**, and **I** will share a conveniently accessible vanishing point. However, while flats **D**, **D2**, **F** and **H** will also share the same vanishing point, it is likely to occur off the drafting board.

Flats **A**, **B**, and **C** rest on grid lines, so their transfer to the perspective grid is strictly visual. Flat **C** conveniently rests in the very middle of a square and is parallel to the orthogonals (fig. 28b). Moving to flat **D**, one can see a dash-line break suggesting an archway. Locate *the entire expanse* of flat **D** as if it were a solid wall. This is to ensure that the alignment of the archway wall will be straight when completed instead of in three, possibly disjointed, sections. The archway itself will get cut into the long wall after the other main walls have been established. Therefore, the joint of **D** to **E** must next be found:

1. On the floor plan, **elongate** flat **D** and note that the elongation strikes the intersection between the fifth transversal and orthogonal (as circled). Locate the same position on the perspective grid and connect with a light line to the upstage end of flat **C** (fig. 28c).
2. On the floor plan, measure the distance from the **center line** to the **D/E** joint. Take this measurement to the perspective grid's

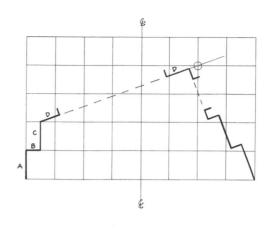

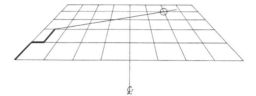

Figure 28c

first transversal and mark its position right of the center line. Push back to the c.v.p. to cross the elongated line (fig. 28d).

Flats D1, D2, and D3 sit behind the D archway and will be located after the main set walls have been established. Flats E, G, and I will share a tangible vanishing point. One may proceed by elongating either E or I. As flat I ends downstage at the very corner of the floor plan grid, it might be wise to find its position first, since its downstage end can be visually plotted. Therefore, elongate I until it crosses the line elongation of D. Transfer this intersection to the perspective grid. On the floor plan measure out from the center line to the intersection of I elongation and D. Transfer this same distance to the perspective grid by measuring right of the center line on the first transversal and making a mark. From the mark, "push back" to the c.v.p. to cross the line elongation of D (fig.

The Perspective Grid

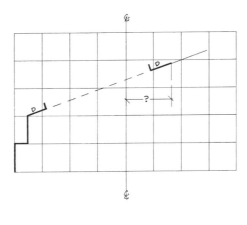

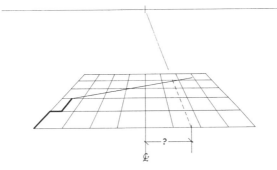

Figure 28d

28e). Once the line elongation of **I** is complete on the perspective grid, align it with a straightedge to cross the horizon line and, thus, find its vanishing point (**V.P.1**). To locate flat **E** on the perspective grid align **V.P.1** with the end of flat **D** and pull a light line downstage.

To find flat **G**, elongate the line of this flat downstage on the floor plan until it crosses the first transversal. Transfer this point to the perspective grid's first transversal, align it with **V.P.1** and extend a light line upstage. What appears now on the grid are the elongated versions of flats **E**, **G** and **I** (fig. 28f). (The doorway in **E** will be found later.)

As flats **F** and **H** share the same outlying vanishing point as flat **D**, their locations can be found by measuring. The quickest way to find flat **F** is to measure its onstage and offstage ends from the floor plan's center line. Take these dimensions to the perspective grid's first transversal and "push back" to the **c.v.p.** Where they cross elongated **E** and elongated **G** will be the two ends of flat **F**. Repeat accordingly to locate flat **H** (fig. 28g).

Expanding the Basics   63

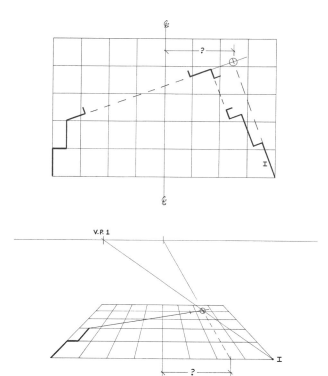

Figure 28e

Let us now return to flats **D1**, **D2**, and **D3**, which make up the window alcove. Locate on the floor plan (and then on the perspective grid) the points where **D1** and **D3** touch flat **D**. On the grid, align these points to **V.P.1** and extend light lines upstage. Locate the upstage end of flat **D1** by measuring out from the floor plan's **center line** and transfer. The upstage end of **D3** rests on the furthest upstage transversal. Connecting the upstage ends of **D1** and **D3** automatically furnishs the ends of flat **D2**, and the basic floor plan is complete (fig. 28h).

The next step is to draw vertical lines up from all of the corners so as to be able to establish the overall heights of the flats and thus provide the shell of the setting. These lines should be light in weight and should extend well above the horizon line (fig. 29).

Let us assume that the height of the set will be 10′. To expedite the measuring process, move to the extreme right (downstage left) vertical line that has been drawn to signify the downstage end of flat **I**. This line

The Perspective Grid

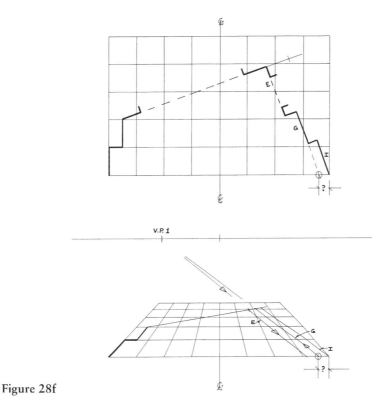

Figure 28f

rests on the first transversal and may be measured directly. Mark off the 10' height on the vertical line. (As this is also an outside line, it will serve as a handy reference for other "pull down" and "push back" needs). Align this mark with **V.P.1** and draw a line to connect with the edge of flat **H**. The overall shape of flat **I** is now complete.

To strike in the tops of flats **G** and **E**, locate where their bottom lines have been extended to cross the first transversal. Lift these points up and draw two light vertical lines at about the 10' high mark. Carry the 10' mark from the top downstage corner of flat **I** to the left with a horizontal guide and make a small hashmark where it crosses the two short vertical lines. From these intersections align with the **c.v.p.** and mark the corresponding top downstage corners of flats **G** and **E**. From these corner heights, align with **V.P.1** and strike in the tops of flats **E** and **G**. The gaps that remain between the top corners of **E** and **G**, and **G** and **I**, may be joined. Thus the tops of **F** and **H** have also been achieved (fig. 30).

Expanding the Basics   65

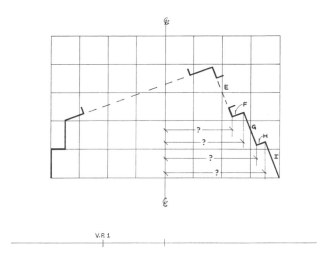

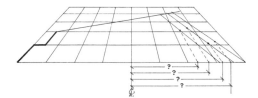

Figure 28g

The stage left height of flat **D** has been automatically found once its joinery to **E** has been established. Now move to flat **A**, find its height, and approach **D** from the other direction. The height of **A** may be found by carrying **I**'s 10′ mark to the left and marking where it hits **A**'s downstage vertical. As flat **A** runs directly on an orthogonal, its vanishing point will be the **c.v.p.** on the grid. Align the 10′ mark with the **c.v.p.** and draw a line until it hits the vertical of flat **B**. And, as **B** runs directly on a transversal, its top can be drawn as a horizontal line. Complete the top of flat **C** as was done with **A**, stopping at the edge of flat **D** (fig. 31). The top of flat **D** can now be drawn by simply connecting the top corners of flats **C** and **E**.

What now appears is the shell of the setting into which the archway and doorway will be cut, and the window alcove will later be seen. Establishing the archway is rather elementary. Measure on the floor plan the distances of the archway sides **i** and **ii** from the **center line** and trans-

The Perspective Grid

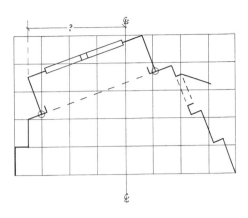

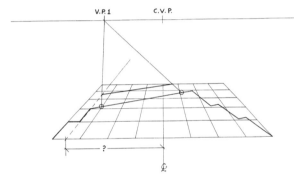

Figure 28h

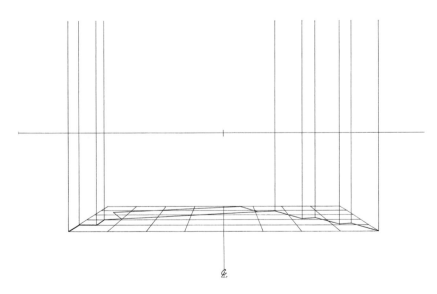

Figure 29

Expanding the Basics

67

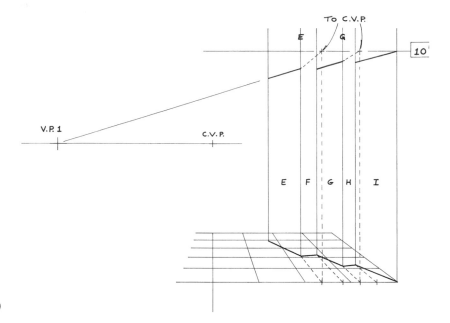

Figure 30

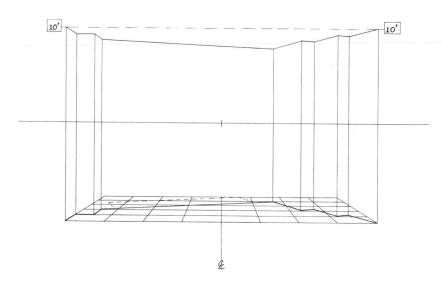

Figure 31

The Perspective Grid

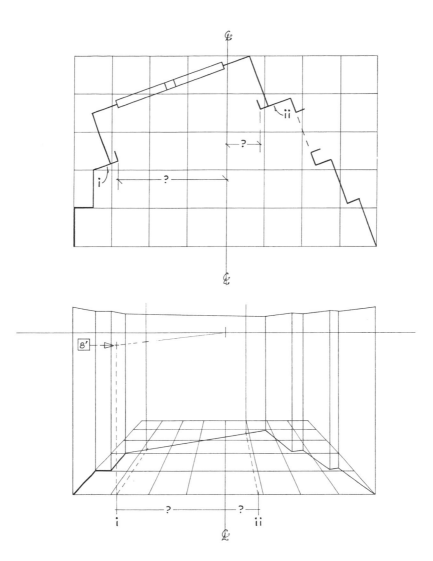

Figure 32a

fer these points to the perspective grid. Draw vertical lines up. The height of the archway must now be found. Choosing an opening 8' high, measure up on the **i** "pull down line" and push back to locate the appropriate height (fig. 32a). Finding the height of **ii** can be done in the same way, but pulling down and pushing back at a point this close to the **center line** necessitate extremely steep angles of relationship to the **c.v.p.** and may result in error.

Expanding the Basics   69

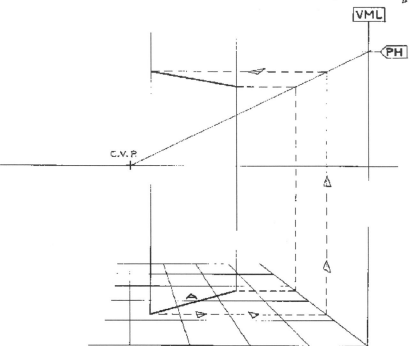

Figure 32b

Consequently, an alternate method for finding the correct height of an object that is close to the **center line** leads us to what, for many, could be considered an easier way to plot *all heights* on the perspective grid.

Shortcut 1

This method involves using a "side wall" approach (fig. 32b) where all common heights are marked on a vertical measuring line (**VML**) placed at the extreme downstage right or left corner of the grid. From each of these marks a line is drawn back to the **c.v.p.** indicating the **perspective height** of an object (**PH**), or **facet** (for example, door height) of an object. For example, to find the 10′ height of wall **A**, the bottom ends, **i** and **ii,** are aligned with the horizontal guide to cross the extreme right orthogonal, then extended directly upward to cross the 10′ **PH** line. These heights are then taken to the left until they cross the vertical

The Perspective Grid

lines that signify the edges of flat **A**, and the 10' height is established. This method is particularly useful for striking walls for which vanishing points cannot be located, and for plotting repetitive molding, doorway, and window heights on the interior setting. All of the common measurements need be marked only once on a single vertical line. Various heights can be found by horizontal and vertical aligning. The degree to which this method may simplify the transfer process depends on the intricacy of the setting itself and, therefore, could prove inconvenient. Ideally, a combination of the "shortcut" and the measuring method would prove the most beneficial.

Accordingly, this side-measuring method should be used whenever the height of an object placed close to the center line must be found, or whenever the task of measuring can be made easier and more accurate.

In figure 33a, the vertical wall thickness (**reveal**) of the archway is parallel with flats **E**, **F**, and **G** and thus shares **V.P.1**. As only one vertical reveal will be seen, extend **ii** toward **V.P.1**. Its depth is then found through floor plan measurement and transfer, and the upstage vertical edge of the reveal is struck. The underside of the arch header will also indicate a reveal as it is placed above eye level. Align the top right corner of the arch opening with **V.P.1** and draw a line that stops at the upstage

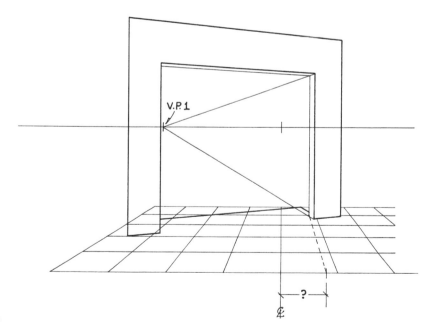

Figure 33a

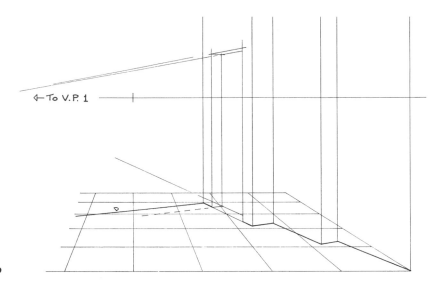

Figure 33b

edge of the vertical reveal. As the reveal on the floor plan is not very deep (and would consequently exhibit little foreshortening), the top arch reveal may be drawn on the perspective grid parallel to the bottom of the header. (If the top reveal were thicker, a difference in slope from the header line would be discernable and therefore the reveal could not be struck as a simple parallel arrangement to the face of the header.)

The door opening in flat **E** is located in the same manner, as the archway from flat **D** and the 7′ high header are drawn in association with **V.P.1**. The bottom of the vertical reveal can be struck in a parallel arrangement with the bottom of flat **D**. Where the vertical reveal meets the top reveal may be struck visually. To indicate the bottom of the door, align the bottom of the vertical reveal with **V.P.1** and draw a line (fig. 33b). Paneling for the door will be dealt with later along with the moldings and trim.

Number 4 on the floor plan indicates a window, but the notation is vague in that it indicates nothing about the window's appearance. All that may be discerned is the division between the windows, which apparently signifies that there are actually two windows of the same width instead of one large window. Begin by establishing the vertical parameters of the opening with the same procedure used for the archway and door. Let us now assume that the bottom of the window opening is 2′ off the floor and that its opening is 5′ high, or 7′ off the floor. Having

The Perspective Grid

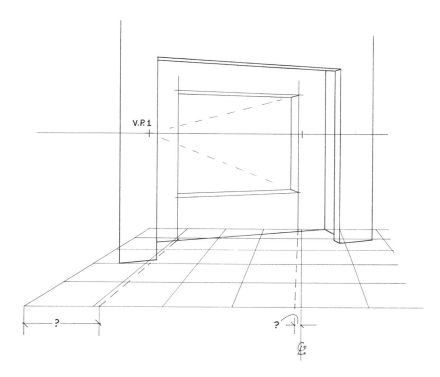

V.P.1

Figure 33c

drawn the window opening, give it a reveal of 6″ (fig. 33c). (This reveal should be drawn *first* on the floor plan, but approximating the 6″ by visual plotting is encouraged.) Note that three reveals will be seen: the vertical one near center stage; the top reveal; and the sill, or bottom reveal.

The division that separates the two equal windows is in the center of the window opening. The center can be found by subdividing ("X-ing") the window opening. At the intersection of the "X," a vertical line is drawn extending through the bottom and top of the window opening. Where this center line hits the opening's top and bottom lines, project lines back to **V.P.1** in order to locate the respective center points on the upstage edges of the reveals (fig. 34a).

The **sash** of the window is the next thing to be drawn. Once the width of the sash has been determined and if its width is not terribly wide (this window features a 3″ sash), the lines indicating the inside edges of the sash may be drawn parallel to the reveal opening. The 3″

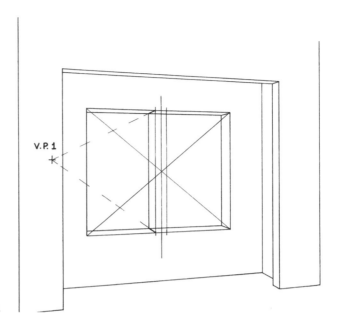

V.P. 1

Figure 34a

Figure 34b

The Perspective Grid

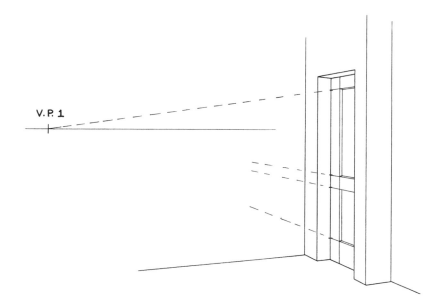

V. P. 1

Figure 35

width was not measured, but only visually estimated: approximately half the width of the 6" vertical reveal was used for comparison. The pieces of wood within the sash are the **mullions** and, depending on their number, may be placed visually. The final touch to the window is expressing the thicknesses of the sash and mullions (fig. 34b).

Adding **panels** to the door shutter is the next step. Approximate the 6" widths of the vertical side boards, or **styles**, through visual reference with the 6" vertical reveal. (Note that only one **style** will be visible as its downstage counterpart is eclipsed by the unseen downstage reveal.) The horizontal top and middle boards will also appear as 6" in width, while the bottom board is 9", or half again as wide as the others. The positions for the horizontal top, middle, and bottom boards are marked on the offstage edge of the vertical reveal where the reveal joins the door. (The middle board is usually centered around the doorknob, which is generally about 3' off the floor.) Align the marks with **V.P.1** and extend the lines across the door. What results is a door with two panels (fig. 35). One can convey at this point if the panels are protruding or recessed depending on whether the boards or the panels have been given reveals. The illustration in figure 35 features recessed panels.

The final touches needed to complete this perspective are the additions of **moldings** and **trim**. Let us first add the trim, or **casings**, around the door and window. Once again, this spacing can be achieved by visual approximation. Very often the width of the casing will match the width of the reveal. Accordingly, both the door and window receive borders that visually correspond to the size of the reveals. The casing may feature further trim, such as applied bead moldings that are drawn parallel to the casing outline, door, window opening, or wherever desired. As the casing is applied to the surface of the wall, it must then protrude from the wall and as such must receive its own reveal. (Note that to indicate the overlap of the casing on the wall, figure 36 shows the bottom line of the face of the door casing extended down slightly and its reveal tapered.)

Most realistic interior settings contain moldings. Depending on the period of the play, one might commonly see a series of three moldings: the **baseboard**, the **chair rail**, and the **cornice**. A simple, yet functional, baseboard containing a top bead can easily be added to the rendering. It looks uniform to have the height of the baseboard approximate the width of the door's bottom horizontal board. Consequently, a 9" mark will be made on the downstage edges of flats **A** and **I**. This height is wrapped from both directions around the set (using the respective vanishing points) until the outside edges of flat **D** have been reached. With a straightedge, connect the height of the baseboards on flat **C** and **E** to draw the molding across the bottom of **D**. Extend the baseboard around the archway reveal using **V.P.1** and on to the alcove flats. To dress up the baseboard, a top **bead** will be added. To do so, visually strike lines slightly below the top line of the baseboard. Give a mitred look to recessed and protruding corners by adding profile shapes. At its cut-off points downstage at the set line, the profile of the entire baseboard is seen (fig. 37).

A **chair rail molding** is practically and aesthetically functional. As its name suggests, its practical purpose is to protect the walls from being scraped by the backs of chairs. Aesthetically, the rail provides visual interest and helps break up large expanses of wall. A 3" band signifying the rail is wrapped around the setting at a height of 3'. The width of the rail will perceptibly diminish as it moves upstage. Therefore, both its top and bottom edges should be drawn using the vanishing points. Any additional lines to suggest the rail's design are to be visually approximated and revealed through the same methods as were practiced on the baseboard. (An additional treatment is shown in figure 38, called

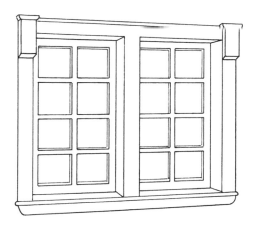

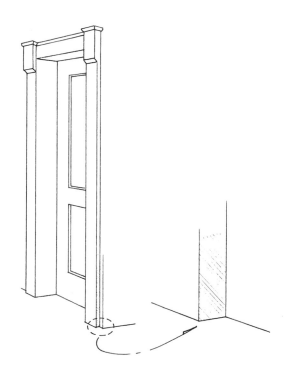

Figure 36

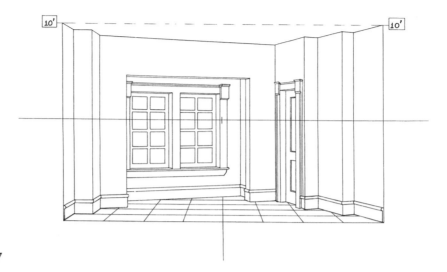

Figure 37

Figure 38

wainscoting. Though the nature of the wainscoting may be quite complex and contain various protruding and recessed panels, a tongue-and-
groove effect is created here by simply adding vertical lines between the
chair rail and baseboard.)

The **cornice molding** is found where the walls would meet the ceil-
ing. It is appropriately found on the realistic interior setting to indicate

The Perspective Grid

Figure 39a

a stopping point for the wall, as many sets will not have ceilings. This molding can be a bit more intricate to draw than the rail or baseboard, especially if it takes a more protruding shape, such as a cove or roman ogee type, or if it features ornate dentil work or the like. Depending, however, on the historical period and the simplicity of the setting, convincing moldings can be drawn with little more effort that it took to draw a baseboard. As the cornice molding is frequently the widest molding in a room (particularly one that is set at a height of 12′), measure down from the top corners along the downstage edges of flats **A** and **I** and wrap this band around the set using the respective vanishing points. Now let us create a molding by enlarging the design for the chair rail: a protruding top bead 3″ wide and a bottom quarter-round cove also 3″ wide. At the same starting points, measure down from the top of the molding 3″ and up from its bottom 3″. Draw the molding's profile shape at the tops of flats **A** and **I** (fig. 39a). Next, wrap the lines of the molding around the set. Note that the top of the molding will run higher than the finished height of the bare walls and that a mitred joinery is suggested to accommodate the molding's shape (fig. 39b).

Assuming the transfer of the basic set is now complete (that is, that no furniture or set dressings will be added), one final step is to be performed: the **verification** of all necessary lines. Ink works well, as its permanence will allow perspective grid lines and all other reference lines

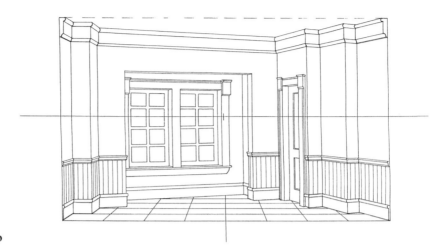

Figure 39b

Figure 40

to be erased after the verification. An inking triangle and a pen housing a 0.1 or 0.2 nib is best so the lines will be dark enough to be visible yet light enough in weight so as to not be overpowering (fig. 40).

Shortcut 2

This simple illustration offers a method that facilitates wall height measuring and that can be expanded to expedite the positioning of

The Perspective Grid

moldings, raised levels, and just about anything that needs to be repeated on both sides of the stage's center line. The two provisions required for this process to work are: (1) the object to be repeated must lie on or within the same depth of plane (or sequence of transversals) occupied by its counterpart on the other side of the stage; and (2) the specifications to be repeated must be of a consistent height off the grid floor.

The floor plan exhibited in figure 41a comprises flats A–I. The stage right run of flats extends further upstage than the stage left run and is made up of flats A–C, with the upstage edge of C placing between transversals 5 and 6. Flats D–I constitute the remainder of the set. The perspective grid in figure 41b indicates the entire floor plan has been transferred:

- The heights of A–C were the first to be drawn, since the remainder of the flats will easily rest within their total plane (or number of transversals).
- Vertical lines marking the joints, or corners, between flats D–I are extended upward, as are the verticals demarcating the down left door.

Establishing the heights of flats D–I will not require any measuring. A horizontal guide and a triangle are all that is needed. It makes no difference whatsoever whether one works first on the downstage flats or the upstage ones, but rather that the triangle and horizontal guide are used in a consistently accurate and secure alignment (fig. 41c):

1. Align the horizontal guide just below the base of the vertical joint between H and I.
2. Move along the straightedge to the left until it hits the base of flat C and make a small mark.
3. With the triangle on the horizontal guide, extend a line from the mark until the top of flat C is crossed. Make another small mark.
4. From the mark at the top of flat C, align to the right using the horizontal guide until the vertical line dividing flats H and I is crossed, and make a third mark. This mark is the correct height at the joint where H and I meet.
5. From the mark on the H and I joint a line is struck to the top of flat C. In doing so the heights of D and H have been established.

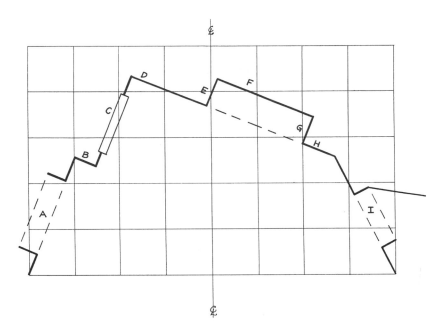

Figure 41a

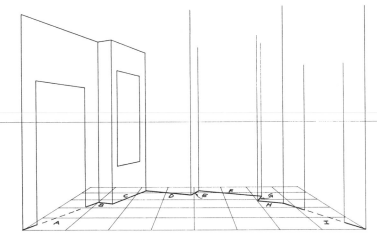

Figure 41b

Figure 41c is, in effect, a version of the "pull down, measure up, push back" scheme ("Shortcut 1," fig. 33b) but the redundancy of measuring has been alleviated. Instead, since the stage right flats had already been measured, they served merely as a guide for simple horizontal and vertical alignment: "slide over, lift up, slide back." Accordingly, the heights

The Perspective Grid

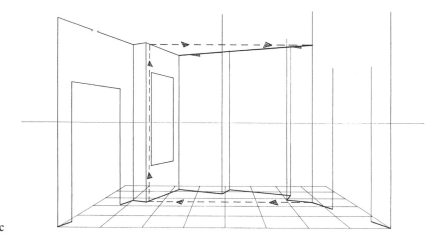

Figure 41c

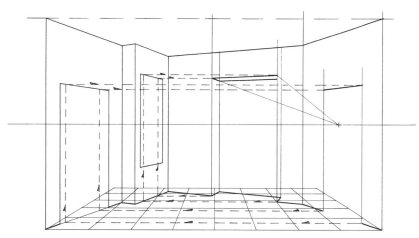

Figure 41d

of flats **D–I** are quickly located through alignment with their stage right counterparts.

Setting the height for the alcove header downstage of flat **F** is quite simple because its overall height is identical to the established window height of flat **C**. The header also conveniently places within the transversal space taken up by the window. Similarly, the downstage left door height is identical to the established height of the downstage right archway (fig. 41d). And, finally, all moldings and trim to be added stage right are easily duplicated stage left using the same "slide over, lift up, slide back" maneuver.

Expanding the Basics

This shortcut method will save truckloads of plotting time and, if performed correctly, will read truly and accurately when checked by individual measuring or alignment with accessible vanishing points. It will prove a particularly expeditious method when transferring the symmetrical setting.

Plotting Curves

Whether one designs graceful archways, resplendent pillars, ornate furniture, castle ruins, or bay windows, **curved lines** are integral to scenic design. They can provide a sweep and elegance to one design while injecting another with frenetic and farcical twists and turns. Up to this point, the use of the perspective grid has been concentrated on the transfer of straight lines, since they easily convey the principles of perspective and foreshortening. There is, after all, an obvious security in the use of straight lines; as long as there are straightedges one can always produce straight lines.

Plotting *curved* platforms and elevations is another matter. A cube may be drawn in perspective as seen from any number of angles. It is simply a matter of measuring schemes, vanishing points, and straightedges; but attempting to draw a circle in perspective can be intimidating. The only way a circle may be seen as a true circle is from straight on! How often will all of the circles needed for a set design be located parallel to the picture plane? Where is the security of the straightedge? Is there not a tool or template that will allow for all of the variables inherent in drawing the "perspective" circle? Unfortunately, there are no ready-made templates or devices available that could possibly cover all angles of placement for circles and curves on the perspective grid.

However, one need not be overly concerned. A circle seen in perspective is actually an **ellipse**. Ellipse templates *do* exist, and with care, such templates may greatly assist the portrayal of circles. Nevertheless, it is likely that only portions of the ellipses found on templates will be used rather than the entire ellipse. The template ellipses are used for scribing circles in isometric drawings and other para-line studies. As para-line drawings do not exhibit any foreshortening and, therefore, are not drawn in perspective (that is, any area of a para-line drawing may be measured to scale) the ellipses on templates are uniform in shape and are not foreshortened. Consequently, for our purposes, segments of el-

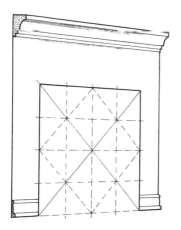
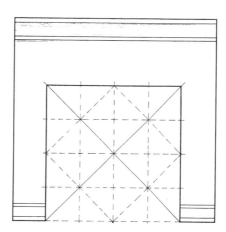

lipses are more likely to be used on the grid than any one entire ellipse shape.

In order to draw circles in perspective using ellipse templates, reference points must be found. A total of twelve (12) points must be located and labeled so as to resemble the face of a clock. (As one becomes more experienced, the number of reference points needed will decrease and the trained eye will take over.) Let's use a circular archway as a drawing example. Of course, the entire arch opening will not be a circle, just its top half, but the entire square opening will be used for reference points. Figure 42a indicates a section of wall drawn in perspective into which a square archway has been cut. To the right of the perspective archway is seen the archway's square opening from the absolute front view:

1. Subdivide the entire openings of both squares with diagonal lines ("X-ing"), and continue subdividing until each is filled with sixteen squares.

Label the ends of all grid lines on the front view as shown in figure 42b. Where the center vertical and horizontal lines meet the outside of the square are four reference points for the circle: **C**, **g**, **c**, and **G**; according to the clockface these points are labeled **12**, **3**, **6**, and **9** (fig. 42b).

2. From the four corners of the outer square, lines are extended to points shown: A to b and f, E to F and d, e to D and H, and a to B and h (fig. 42c). To put it another way, the outside four squares making up each perimeter side of the overall square are

Expanding the Basics   85

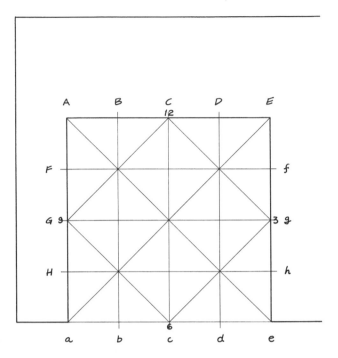

Figure 42b

treated like a long rectangle. Each of the long rectangles is then subdivided. These subdividing lines will be used to locate the remaining reference points.

3. The remaining reference points (or numbers on the clockface) needed to scribe a circle can be found where each subdiving line (as in 2, above) moves inward from the perimeter square's corner and first intersects vertical and horizontal lines. These points are indicated by hollow dots and labeled **1, 2, 4, 5, 7, 8, 10,** and **11** (fig. 42d).

4. As only the top half of the circle is needed to form the archway, the hollow dots corresponding to the clockface numbers **9, 10, 11, 12, 1, 2,** and **3** are now connected to form the circle (fig. 42e).

At this juncture, connecting the relative points on the perspective grid's archway grid might give one pause. Attempting to draw the connections freehand are apt to appear as just that: drawn freehand. To

The Perspective Grid

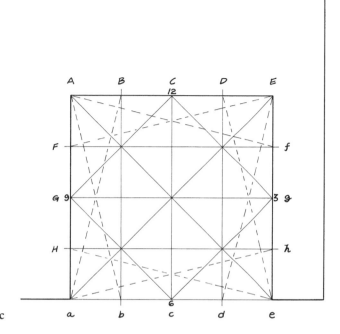

Figure 42c

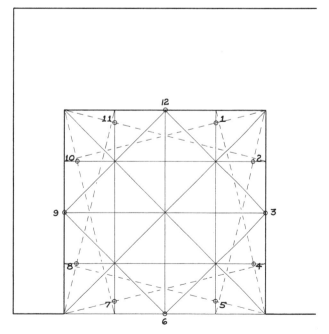

Figure 42d

Expanding the Basics

87

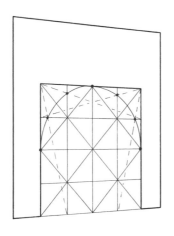 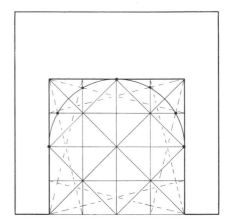

Figure 42e

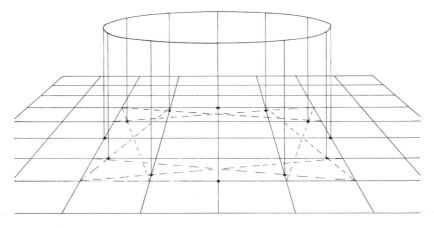

Figure 43

duplicate the crispness of straight lines, search through available ellipse and circle templates. Attempt to match the sweep of their curved cut-outs with the reference points on the drawing. Then use the relevant sections of the templates to scribe the curves. For larger circles and sweeps, experiment with several **french curves.**

NOTE: Although a square opening was used for this exercise the *same* subdividing and clockface procedure would be followed for scribing an ellipse within a rectangular opening.

The above procedure is the same one used to draw a horizontal circle (for example, a circular platform). Reference points are found on the floor plan of the perspective grid, and if need be, each number on the

The Perspective Grid

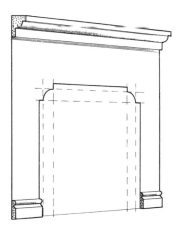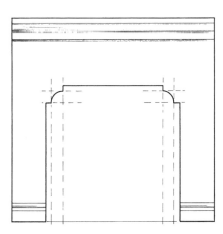

Figure 44

clockface is projected up to the intended height and is connected (fig. 43). Circular tabletops may also be found in the same way, though their proportionately smaller sizes usually necessitate fewer reference points. (See "Furniture," below).

Occasionally, one may need to draw an archway whose corners are curved but whose base of the header is a straight horizontal line (fig. 44). In that case, the drawing is considerably easier and faster to do than the 180° circular arch outlined above. On a separate sheet, quickly draw a scaled front elevation of the unit. Measure where the quarter circles in the corners are placed. That is, define how far up the side of the arch the circle begins and how far into the arch the curvature ends. Transfer these points to the square arch opening on the perspective grid. Rarely, unless the arch motif is complex, should any additional reference points be needed. With the aid of an ellipse or circle template strike in the curves.

The importance of using templates as drawing aids to create perspective curves cannot be overstated. Nothing looks worse on a perspective rendering than a tentative use of line. Most people are simply incapable of drawing fluidly curving lines in perspective and the use of a drawing aid, combined with established reference points, is practically essential in order to produce a presentation-quality appearance. Become familiar with all of your templates and experiment to learn both their proper usage and the many unorthodox ways they can be used for invaluable assistance.

Expanding the Basics   89

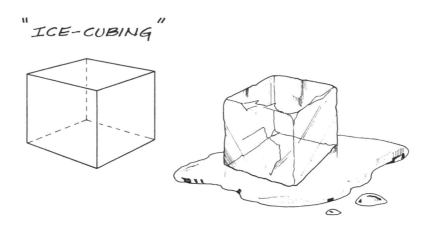

Figure 45

Creating Levels

A **level** traditionally refers to an area raised above the stage floor that will support the weight of actors and is therefore to be used as an acting area. Nearly every stage setting contains levels of some kind. They may exist for dramatic reasons, architectural justification, sightline considerations, or merely visual interest, and can take the form of raised rooms, entrance landings, steps, staircases, or ramps.

Drawing raised levels on the perspective grid is no different in concept and procedure than drawing a single flat of a designated height. A box, for instance, is really a joining of four short walls that, when put together with a lid, forms a three-dimensional structure. The only thing that differentiates the box from the single wall is the addition of the other three walls needed to create the box's appearance.

NOTE: Before the finished shape of a level is verified, the lines used to create that three-dimensional structure (for example, fig. 45) often look somewhat like a sophisticated version of a child's drawing of an ice cube. Being transparent, the ice cube allows us to see its base and back corner. In effect, raised levels start out as drawings of ice cubes and the verification of selected lines eventually renders the ice cube opaque. Consequently, to render three-dimensional objects effectively it is often necessary to "ice-cube" a drawing so as to reveal relevant reference points.

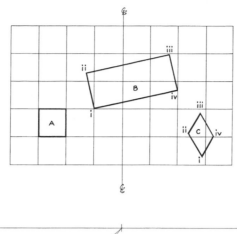

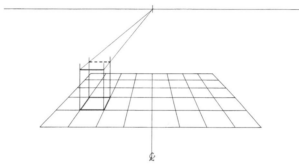

Figure 46a

Figure 46a shows three arrangements of levels. Notice that, regardless of the intended height of a level, its overall shape was first drawn on the perspective grid's floor and then its corners were elevated to a specified height. Level **A** rests on grid lines and both its front and rear faces are parallel to transversals, while the sides are parallel to orthogonals and adhere to the **c.v.p.** When a unit is placed thus, only the height of one of the two downstage corners needs to be located. The remainder of the level, or box, is completed using horizontal and vanishing point lines.

The base of level **B** was located by visual reference and line elongations. The side of the level aligned most severely toward upstage (corner **i** to corner **ii**) converges to a tangible vanishing point. Whenever vanishing points for levels can be found, the amount of measuring required to establish that level's height is half the amount of measuring that

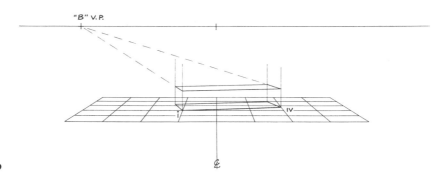

Figure 46b

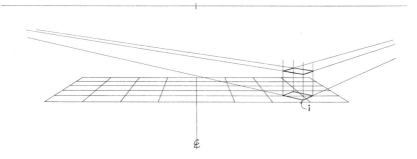

Figure 46c

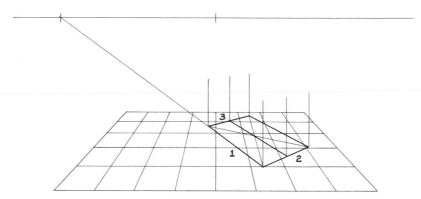

Figure 47a

would be required for a level not affiliated with vanishing points. The heights of corners **i** and **iv** were found separately, and these heights were projected back to corners **ii** and **iii**, respectively. To finish the top of the level requires joining corner **i** with **iv**, and **ii** with **iii** (fig. 46b).

All too infrequently, a level may be conveniently shaped so as to affiliate with two or more accessible vanishing points. For this pleasant rar-

The Perspective Grid

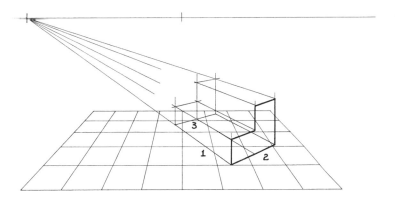

Figure 47b

ity, as demonstrated by level **C** (fig. 46c), the height of only one corner need be found. One would usually locate the height of the corner furthest downstage (**i**) and simply wrap this height around the object using the vanishing points and thereby create the raised surface.

Not always is a level raised to only one height. Figure 47a illustrates a two-tiered surface. The height separation between the two tiers could occur anywhere, but here it is shown to occur as dividing the structure straight down the middle. This was done to further illustrate the subdividing procedure. Once the structure's perimeter shape was established, diagonal lines drawn from corner to corner revealed the middle of the base. The diagonal intersection was aligned with the affiliate vanishing point (relating to side **1**) and the line signifying the tier separation on the floor of the grid was struck. The profile shape of the object (side **2**) was the next to be drawn: lines were taken to the vanishing point, the heights of side **3** were projected up from the grid floor to meet the vanishing point lines, and the structure was complete (fig. 47b).

To create a ramp (as shown in fig. 48a) merely requires elevating one end of the level and not the other. The steps shown in figure 48b were raised to predetermined heights and expeditiously aligned with vanishing points.

When drawing a composite arrangement of several levels it is best to first establish the height of the highest level. Because this would normally be the platform furthest upstage, all subsequent lower levels may then be placed against the facing of the upper level or in lower relationships to it. Attempting to begin by plotting the heights of lower downstage levels prior to establishing higher upstage ones will increase the

Expanding the Basics   93

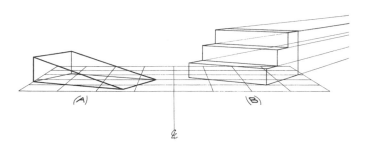

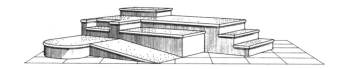

Figure 49

amount of "ice-cubing" and force one to constantly "see through" one level to get to the next; the transfer process becomes unnecessarily complicated.

Levels used in interior settings or for an elaborate courtyard or piazza often have finished moldings at their top edges. While some moldings will be more complex than others, even the simplest of bullnosing adds an attractive finishing touch to units that might otherwise appear austere. Unless straight, lengthy expanses of molding are required, the artist may generally strike lines parallel to, and just below, the top edge of the level to be decorated. When the molding extends to the corner of the platform a simple profile of the molding is drawn. If vanishing points for the levels exist, they should be used to strike the molding lines (fig. 49).

Furniture

Because furniture contains a significant amount of detail, it is more difficult to draw on the perspective grid than other scenic objects. The first guideline, then, to rendering a piece of furniture in perspective is to attempt to capture, within reason, its *spirit*. The perimeter lines and allusions to detail will suffice. Striving to duplicate pressed wood, carvings, brocade fabric, or braided fringe will lead to enormous frustration and is unnecessary, since minute detail on the standard ½" scale will not read.

The second guideline, which is irrefutable, is that furniture must initially be drawn in block, geometric form. For example, regardless how padded or stuffed the end result of a chair is to be, the *beginnings* of the furniture unit must be formulated around overall dimensions that initially render a boxlike appearance. The padding is usually drawn freehand (based on established geometric parameters), which gives the piece a sense of normalcy and visual comfort. Of course, should one be drawing modern or clinical furniture more of a reliance will be placed on straightedges and templates in order to keep lines precise and give the furniture a "clean" look.

To illustrate a procedure for drawing furniture, refer to the example of the sofa shown in figure 50 that began as a small rectangular platform. This platform conforms to the specified length, width, and height needed for the design, and it may be built from scratch, pulled or adapted from an existing stock piece, or simply reflect the dimensions of an item to be purchased or borrowed. Added to the base are a rectangular backrest and two rectangular armrests, and slots at the bottom front and side have been inserted to indicate the leg placements. These geometric shapes reflect the overall size of the sofa unit and the spaces within which its specific shapes and attributes are to be drawn. Revised shapes are lightly sketched within the geometric parameters, and templates are used as needed to assist fluidities in line. Vanishing points are

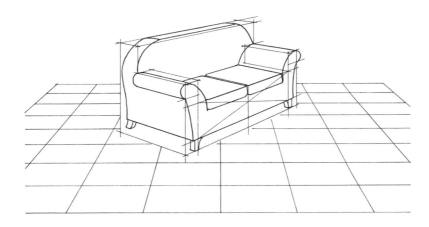

Figure 50

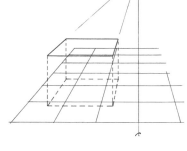

DISTANCE IS APPROX. 1/3 OF RADIUS

Figure 51a, b, c

consulted where applicable. When all is drawn to satisfaction, the entire unit is **verified**.

Drawing a circular table in perspective will often require the designer to make use of his or her own visual sense of proper appearance in order to achieve an effective look of foreshortening. One may, of course, plot the circular tabletop using the above method for plotting curves, but because tabletops are commonly parallel to the floor (or appear as level) their "flat" position makes the locating of the many circle reference points difficult to discern. One would be better off to approximate a few simply located points of reference.

Begin by plotting the circle as a square table with the **c.v.p.** as a principal reference point. Elevate the overall square within which the circular tabletop is to appear to its playing height (fig. 51a). Next, **subdivide** the square area of the tabletop as shown in figure 51b. The four reference points (3, 6, 9, and 12 o'clock) are dotted. On the downstage edge

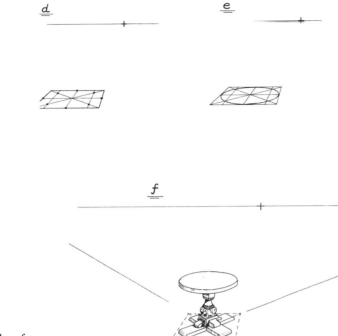

Figure 51d, e, f

of the square tabletop, locate points approximately one-third of the distance from the outside edges of the table to the table's center line, or 6 o'clock. Carry these points upstage in alignment with the **c.v.p.** (fig. 51c).

Where these extended lines cross the original "X" subdivision of the square table, four additional points are located (fig. 51d). These four additional points are meant to serve as an approximate guide or ballpark placement for the circular sweep. Sketching freehand, the points (or their approximate positions) are connected and when the illusion of the tabletop appears credible sections of templates may be found to assist in the verification.

NOTE: One ellipse from an ellipse template cannot be used to scribe the entire table top as the template ellipse is not cut in perspective. Rather, portions of several ellipses, or circles, may need to be combined in order to complete the table top (fig. 51e).

The pedestal base and legs of the table are geometrically plotted and designs drawn within to complete the furniture unit (fig. 51f).

Other pieces, such as the buffet and sideboard illustrated in figure 52, rely a bit more heavily on geometric beginnings as many of those

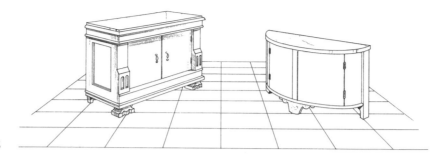

Figure 52

"beginnings" will actually become the lines of the unit with only subtle variations. In time, the artist will learn to depend more heavily on his or her sense of proportion and perspective. Both of these units reflect a balanced blend of drafting-assisted and freehand drawing methods.

Furniture makes an invaluable contribution to a setting not only for the sake of visual interest but in a communicative sense as well. The nature and style of the furniture offers information as to the period of the play and often goes beyond an economic statement to furnish information about the play's characters. And, from both a dramatic and pragmatic standpoint, furniture is arranged on the stage so as to facilitate or substantiate stage business. This usually requires that furniture be placed in groupings or "conversational areas" that, for blocking variety, can be approached from several directions. As such, pieces may need to be placed away from walls to allow for easy access. To accommodate versatility in movement patterns, more than one conversational area is commonly needed. Accordingly, when placing furniture in the perspective rendering one must be acutely aware of visual overlaps. An end table might cover part of a chair, just as a sofa will likely eclipse a portion of wall.

When verifying the rendering (particularly ink verification) be especially careful to verify first that which is placed farthest downstage, that is, nearest the observer. Some renderings become so complex with line notations, "ice-cubings," and such, that artists frequently need to verify something in order to keep track of their work. Nothing should be verified unless first checked for its overlapping status. When painting with watercolor washes there are few things more frustrating than inking a section of drawing only to realize that a sofa will be sitting directly downstage of what has just been verified! To make matters worse, the sofa must now be painted with an opaque medium to cover up unintended lines and, because of the difference in treatment, the visual unity of the rendering is disrupted.

It is no wonder that the verification stage gives artists more pause than any other step in the perspective grid process!

5. The Perspective Grid: Variations

Up to this point, all that has been covered has related to challenges encountered when transferring an interior setting to the perspective grid. Transferring an exterior setting involves much the same points and concerns, particularly where buildings, curbs, bridges, and so on, are glimpsed. However, many exterior designs will include products of nature, such as trees, foliage, distant hillsides, and the like. Although these elements, when faithfully drawn, may depart from hardline drafting principles, they all should logically begin with a geometric parameters. All scenic elements must have their overall size and shape established before their individually unique characteristics may be drawn. So, in theory, there is little difference in the transfer process between a straightforward interior or exterior setting.

Straightforward is perhaps an artistically contentious term. Nothing in theatrical design should be "straightforward"; the word implies "mundane." Each setting should be special to that one particular play and not suffice for any number of plays. Settings may be extravagant or minimalist, captivating or boring, but never "straightforward." However, each of the exercises illustrated thus far has been straightforward in the sense that floors are flat, walls are geometric, and the downstage edge of the set has taken the form of a set line rigidly parallel to the picture plane.

Departing from these limitations indisputably allows for a greater freedom of design expression and affords the setting a different level of contribution to the dramatic expression. Settings that were once formalized by the dictates of realism take on added meaning as they jut toward the audience space or seem to rest precariously on tipped levels.

100

To enhance and expand one's understanding of the perspective grid and glimpse some of its inherent varieties and possibilities for expressive design, the following will undertake the challenges unique to transferring the thrust and raked stages.

The Thrust Stage

The thrust stage does as the name implies: it thrusts forward toward the observer and breaks the hard setline that is found in designs done in the traditional proscenium-arch style. The thrust stage can offer a greater sense of intimacy for the audience because it brings players further downstage than traditionally afforded. Often, interesting lower levels are incorporated in the thrust in order to not only maximize sightline possibilities, but also to heighten dramatic impact.

The manner in which the floor plan is initially gridded greatly determines the eventual effect of the rendering. One may place the grid on the floor plan in either of two ways. The first way would be to set the first transversal at the downstage extremity of the thrust (fig. 53a). On the one hand, this negates having to "add" a thrust to the perspective grid, while on the other hand, it relegates detailed, upstage parts of the set (that usually contain the majority of the flats in a thrust setting) to the farthest transversals on the perspective grid. Even the beginner realizes it is easier to transfer details to the downstage areas of the grid than to the upstage areas.

The second way to orient the floor plan grid is to place the first transversal at either the edge of the permanent stage or at a downstage point where the main set elevation ends (fig. 53b). Some designs may have a set line where one or both halves of the elevation end. While in this second orientation the thrust will have to be added downstage of the perspective grid, the majority of detail work and elevations will begin placement on the first transversal and thus ease the transfer process. It is this second method of floor plan grid placement that will be covered, since the first method does not truly constitute a thrust arrangement but only a hugely extended, upstage treatment of customary perspective-grid procedures.

Whether one moves upstage or downstage of the perspective grid's first transversal, one important factor remains constant: *One may measure only in association with the first transversal*. It may be measured to

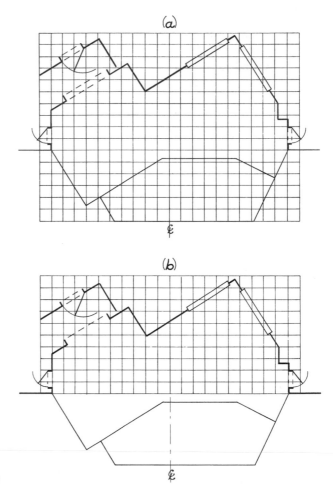

Figure 53a, b

the right or left, or up or down. All measurements along this line are either pushed back or, in the case of the thrust stage, pulled forward.

Refer to the floor plan of the thrust in figure 54a. For simplicity of illustration it is symmetrical not only in shape but in placement: it is virtually centered on the center line of the stage. Therefore, only one-half of the thrust need be located, as the other half will be repeated and placed by merely locating measured reference points and connecting them. The shape of the thrust is marked by letters at its corners. Points **A** and **B** are located on the first transversal, while **C** and **D** mark the downstage extremities. Moving to the perspective grid in figure 54b:

The Perspective Grid

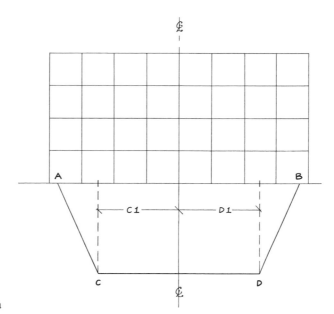

Figure 54a

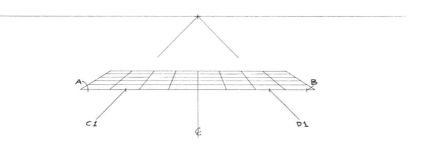

Figure 54b

1. **A** is located by measuring out from the center line on the first tranversal of the floor plan and finding the corresponding points on the perspective grid. Repeat this procedure for **B**.
2. The distance of point **C** from the center line is first measured on the floor plan and then transferred to the first transversal of the perspective grid where it is marked. This mark is aligned with the **c.v.p.** and pulled forward in a light line, noted **C1**. Repeat this procedure to strike **D** and **D1**.

The placement of point **C** (stage right of the center line) has now been established, but its distance downstage of the first transversal has not.

Variations   103

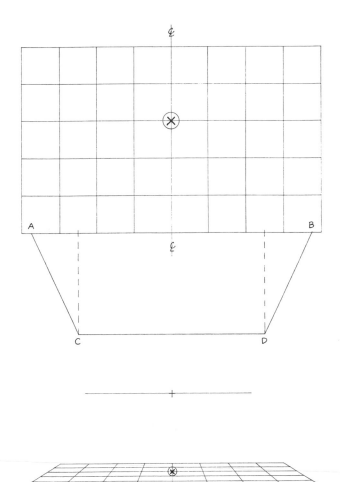

Figure 54c

This distance can be measured on the floor plan but not on the perspective grid. To find the position of **C** on **C1** of the perspective grid:

3.   It is necessary to establish a reference point on both the floor plan and the perspective grid. On the floor plan, make an **x** where the center line intersects with the fourth transversal. Find its counterpart on the perspective grid and make another **x** (fig. 54c).

The Perspective Grid

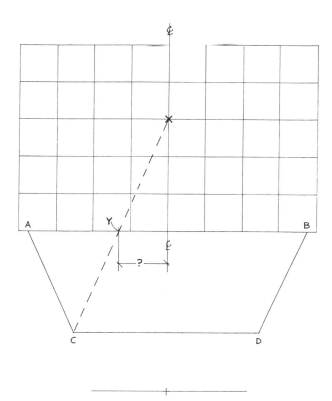

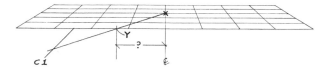

Figure 54d

4. On the floor plan, align **x** with **C**, and where the straightedge crosses the first transversal make a **y**. Measure the distance from **y** to the **CL**.
5. Transfer this distance to the perspective grid by measuring along the first transversal to the left of the center line and make a mark (fig. 54d).
6. On the perspective grid, align **x** with **y** and extend the straight-

Figure 54e

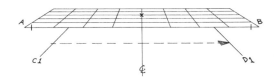

Figure 54f

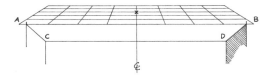

Figure 54g

edge until it crosses line **C1**. At this intersection will be point **C** of the thrust (fig. 54e).

7. Point **D** is found by extending a horizontal line to the right from the point where **C** crosses **D1** (fig. 54f).

8. Connect and verify **A** to **C**, **C** to **D**, and **D** to **B**. Extend vertical lines downward from corners **A**, **B**, **C**, and **D** to indicate the mass of the thrust structure (fig. 54g).

The above thrust is meant to be an extension of the same level as the stage floor, or +0" elevation. Creating a thrust that is lower than the stage floor is an elementary procedure. Figure 55a indicates that at points **A** and **Y** (that is, where point **C** is extended upstage to cross the

The Perspective Grid

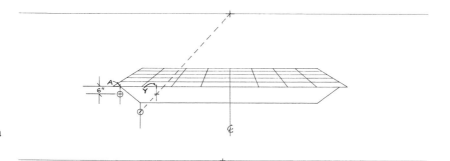

Figure 55a

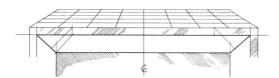

Figure 55b

first transversal), lines are dropped straight down from the first transversal and marked at a depth of 6", or, in effect, at the −6" level. (Any elevation on the stage that is *lower than the permanent stage floor* is listed in the minus category, for example, −6", −12", −18", and so on.) As **A** is placed at the first transversal, its lowered position is automatically established. The −6" drop on **Y** is aligned with the **c.v.p.** and pulled forward. Find the respective points of **B** and **D**, connect the points as above, and verify (fig. 55b).

The thrust floor plan pictured in figure 56a is asymmetrical in shape and, aside from the fact that two downstage corners must be located instead of one, is no more difficult to draw than the above symmetrical thrust. Figure 56b shows how the thrust was transferred to the perspective grid and the steps as numbered in the symmetrical thrust transfer have been repeated and labeled to show their use in this transfer.

Rarely is a thrust of any appreciable size integrated into a design without there being a piece (or pieces) of furniture placed upon it. The furniture might take the form of a garden or courtyard bench or stool and generally accommodates actor blocking concerns, stage business, or the need for variation in levels. Any backrest on the furniture is either nonexistent or kept very low for sightline considerations. Drawing furniture on a thrust is not nearly as difficult as it might at first seem. The

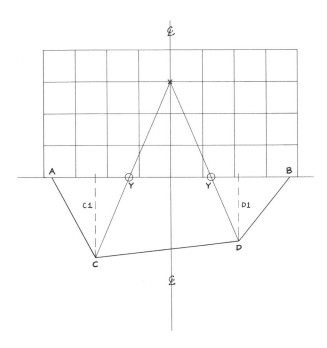

Figure 56a

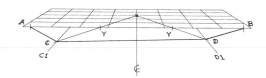

Figure 56b

placement of furniture can be accurately measured and is based on the procedure of **line elongation**. In fact, once one learns how to draw one piece of furniture on the thrust, one should be able to draw *any* piece on the thrust. The procedures that establish a unit of furniture's position and height are constant; the variables are the specifics of its size and the degree of embellishment.

The asymmetrical-thrust floor plan pictured in figure 57a features an 18" high block placed upon the thrust. The first thing one should observe is that the stage right side of the block, that is, the edge joining corners **i** and **ii**, is *parallel* to the stage right edge of the thrust. Therefore,

The Perspective Grid

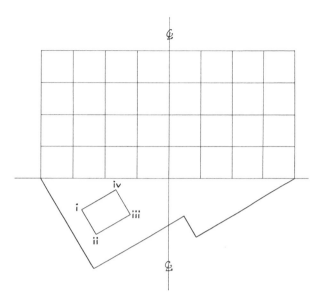

Figure 57a

both the block and that edge of the thrust will share the same **vanishing point**:

1. On the floor plan, extend lines along the two sides of the block upstage until they cross the first transversal. Mark these two points and measure their placement out from the center line (fig. 57b).

2. Place corresponding marks, **A** and **B**, on the first transversal of the perspective grid. Extend the stage right edge of the thrust so as to locate its V.P. (**V.P.1**) on the horizon line (fig. 57c).

3. Align **V.P.1** with **A** and pull a light line downstage (line elongating) from the first transversal onto the thrust. Repeat with **B**.

The two light lines pulled downstage onto the thrust indicate the planes of the right and left sides of the block. Establishing the four corners of the block, **i, ii, iii,** and **iv,** will determine its upstage and downstage sides and place it in its proper position. To locate corner **i:**

4. On the floor plan, measure the distance between **i** and the first orthogonal of the floor plan grid. Transfer this distance to the first transversal on the perspective grid and make an **x** (fig. 57d).

Variations   109

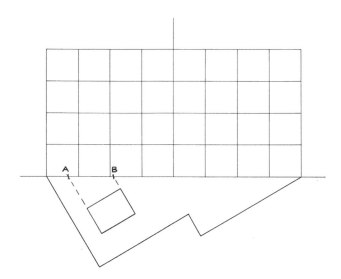

Figure 57b

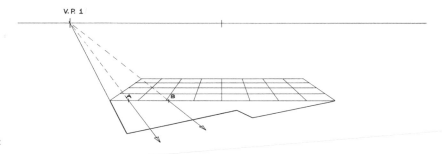

Figure 57c

5. Align a straightedge with the **c.v.p.** and **x**. Where the straight-edge continues downstage and crosses the **line elongation** of **A** will be corner **i**. *Repeat this procedure* to find **ii**, and then use the **B line elongation** to locate **iii** and **iv** (fig. 57e).

6. Joining **i** to **iv** and **ii** to **iii** will establish the upstage and down-stage edges, respectively (fig. 57f).

The base of the block is complete. Now its height must be found.

7. Extend light vertical lines up from each of the block's four corners.

8. Extend light vertical lines up from **A** and **B**, measure up to heights of 18" and make marks **AH** and **BH**. Align **V.P.1** with

The Perspective Grid

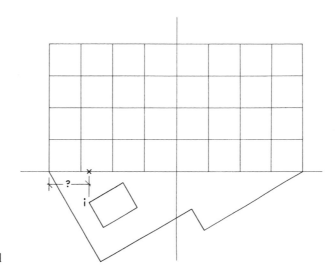

Figure 57d

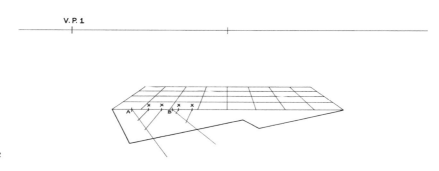

V. P. 1

Figure 57e

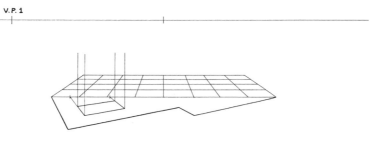

V. P. 1

Figure 57f

Variations   111

AH and **BH** and pull downstage to cross through vertical corner lines **i, ii, iii,** and **iv** (fig. 57g).

9. Complete the block's top surface by connecting top corners **i** to **iv** and **ii** to **iii** (fig. 57h).

Though the above transfer was expedited with an accessible vanishing point, placing a unit on a thrust without the aid of a vanishing point is really no more difficult a procedure, albeit a slightly more time-consuming one. Fortunately, the number of units placed on the thrust is usually quite low, and compared with the floor area of the grid, the thrust is normally free from numerous lines and notations. And, regardless of the number of vanishing points or measuring notations, note that one constant keeps popping up whether elements are drawn on the stage floor or the surface of the thrust: the base of the object (the block, above) is *always* drawn first before its height is established. Even if a thrust drops below +0" and furniture sits upon it, all is drawn as if to appear to extend from the level of the stage on a sheet of clear glass and then points are dropped or raised as needed (fig. 58).

The Raked Stage

A **raked** stage is one that slopes. Instead of a level stage or platform, the raked acting area will pitch down toward the audience in either one main decline or a series of declines. A stage may be raked for a variety of dramatic and artistic reasons, to pique visual interest, or simply for sightline considerations. Sometimes the entire acting area is composed of one giant rake, while at other times individual platforms may cascade at differing angles. Sometimes only the thrust will be sloped. Whatever the rationale for its existence or its shape, a **raked stage** offers unique challenges to both actor and designer.

The most comfortable (or most easily negotiable) rake upon which to act drops on the average of 1′ every 8′. With this degree of pitch the acting floor looks almost level from the audience's view. For more dramatic import some rakes may have slopes as steep as 15°, which translates to a drop of a little over 2′ to the 8′ span! Such a decline makes a strong visual statement but can be a safety hazard to performers.

The transfer of the raked stage to the perspective grid offers unique challenges but provides rewarding and captivating visual results. Even

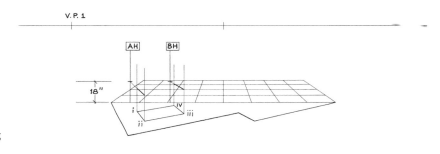

Figure 57g

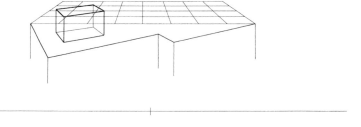

Figure 57h

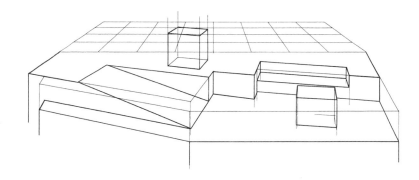

Figure 58

though an entire acting area may be raked, the tops of the furniture that rests upon it are normally level, and the combination of the two plane variations invites substantial visual and dramatic interest.

A form of the raked stage in perspective has already been discussed, albeit briefly. A sloping surface that occurs on the grid floor is treated

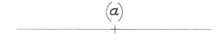

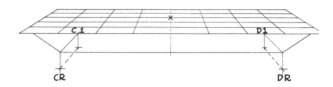

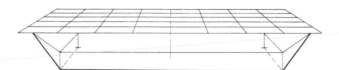

Figure 59a, b

in the same manner as one would draw a ramp; perhaps the platform to be transferred may have a greater variety in shape or angle of decline than a standard ramp, but the plotting of its shape and the heights of its corners is a fairly straightforward operation. Even transferring the raked **symmetrical thrust** should be a simple matter and not pose a transfer problem (Rake I, fig. 59a). Instead of locating the two downstage corners at +0", drop the first transversal reference points of **C1** and **D1** down 12" (actually −12", as the first transversal is located at +0"), align the drop-downs with the grid's **c.v.p.** and pull the −12" drop forward to the thrust's downstage corner lines, **CR** and **DR**. Connect the dropped-down corners with the upstage corners (**A** and **B**) placed at +0" and the raked thrust is complete (fig. 59b).

The Perspective Grid

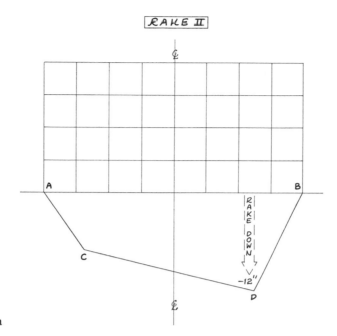

Figure 60a

Transferring the raked **asymmetrical thrust** and that which rests upon it requires an additional view in order to correctly draw in perspective: the **cross section** (**x-sect**). Rake II, shown in figure 60a, is a relatively elementary thrust rake. Points **A** and **B** adjoin the first transversal and are at +0". Point D, the lowest tip of the rake at −12", is not a problem to plot as evidenced by the above symmetrical example. However, because Rake II is not symmetrical in shape, point **C** does not extend as far downstage as point **D** and therefore does not drop down as low. In order to establish the height (or drop) of **C**, a **scaled cross section** must be drawn that shows the permanent stage (**ps**), the decline of the rake, and the extent of the rake's downstage projection (fig. 60b). *Note that both the vertical line signifying the edge of the stage (**SE**) and the horizontal line indicating +0" (**GZ**) have been included in the cross section.* The downstage extremity of the rake (point **D**) is established by measuring out from **SE** along **GZ**, then dropped on a vertical line to a depth of −12". A diagonal line is then drawn from **D** to **SE** to show the rake pitch (**RP**).

Rake II is transferred as if it were a level thrust. Point D is dropped down to −12" (fig. 60c). To locate the drop of **C**:

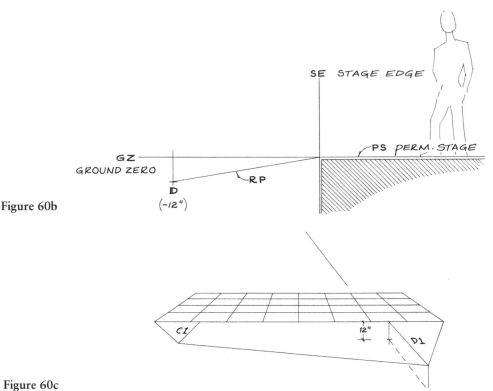

Figure 60b

Figure 60c

1. On the floor plan of the thrust, measure the distance of **C** from the edge of the stage (fig. 60d).

2. Transfer this distance to the **x-sect** by measuring from **SE** to the left along **GZ** (thus out over the raked thrust), and mark **C**. Extend a vertical line down to **RP** (fig. 60e).

3. Measure the drop-down from **GZ** to **RP** and transfer this measurement to the perspective grid. Drop down point **C** to this dimension. Connect **A** and **B** with respective drop-downs **C** and **D** to complete the raked thrust (fig. 60f).

The bench in figure 61a is portrayed on the perspective grid as a flat projection overhanging the raked thrust. Note that the four corners of the bench have vertical lines extended through them and the corners have been labeled **i–iv** to explain the transfer. An accessible vanishing point (**V.P.1**) was found. The height of the bench will be established at +15″ above its lowest base point on the rake. However, because the

116   *The Perspective Grid*

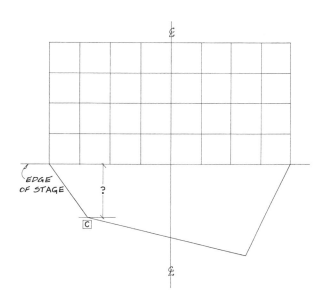

Figure 60d

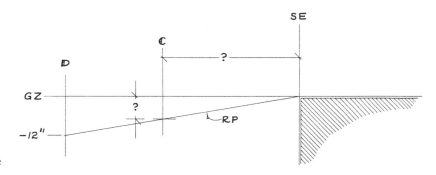

Figure 60e

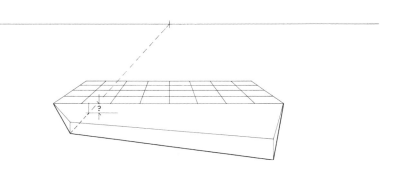

Figure 60f

Variations

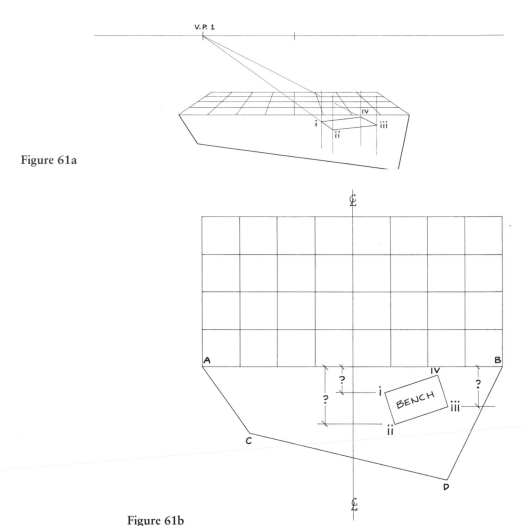

Figure 61a

Figure 61b

bench rests on a thrust that rakes to below **GZ,** *the bench must first be plotted on the cross section* before its transfer to the perspective grid may begin.

Refer to the floor plan of the bench (fig. 61b). Corner **iv** of the bench will not be seen. Measuring corners **i–iii** downstage from the first transversal is the beginning step. Next, transfer these three lateral dimensions to the same **cross section** used to draw the rake:

The Perspective Grid

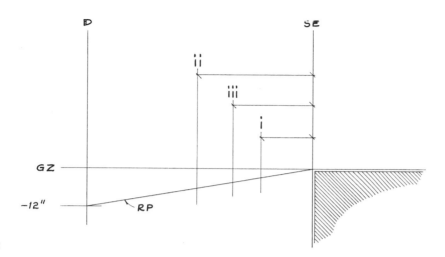

Figure 61c

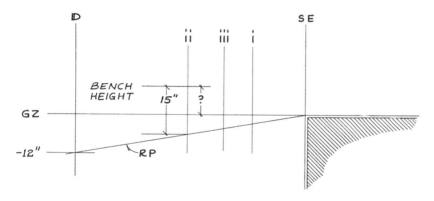

Figure 61d

1. Plot corners **i, ii,** and **iii** along **GZ** and extend vertical lines down through to **RP** as shown (fig. 61c).
2. As **ii** is the furthest downstage corner of the bench, measure upward from **RP** to a height of 15" and make a mark. Measuring *down* from this mark to line **GZ** will now furnish the height of the bench above **GZ** (fig. 61d).

This height may now be transferred to the perspective grid in order to complete the top of the bench, as assisted by **V.P.1.** Nevertheless, what provides the illusion of the rake is the appearance of the *bottom* of the bench as it rests upon the surface of the rake.

Variations

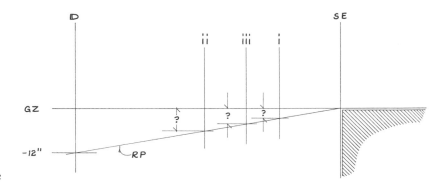

Figure 61e

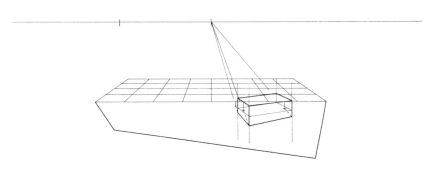

Figure 61f

3. At the **x-sect**, measure and notate the distances corners **i**, **ii**, and **iii** drop below **GZ** to hit **RP** (fig. 61e).

4. Transfer the distances from step 3 to the perspective grid, locate the dropped corners and **verify** (fig. 61f).

Occasionally, a rake will continue from a low point on the thrust to a high point upstage above **GZ**. The coded floor plan in fig. 62a presents a raised level of +18" that covers most of the stage and part of the thrust. The high point of the rake occurs 6′ upstage of the first transversal at a height of +12", and the rake slopes to a downstage low point of −9". Two steps, one +12" and the other +6", allow access between the main-stage level and the rake, while downstage left is a seat +10" in height above **GZ**. All of the facets of the floor plan are transferred to the perspective grid and heights/drop-downs are ready to be assigned (fig. 62b). The various features on the floor plan have been transferred to a **cross section** (fig. 62c).

The Perspective Grid

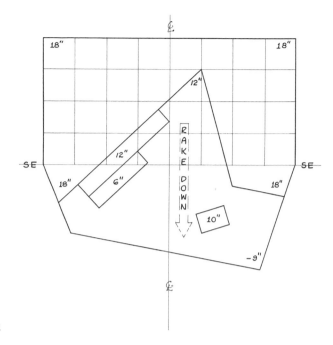

Figure 62a

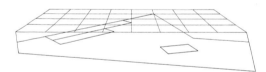

Figure 62b

Normally, all of these measurements and transfers to the cross section would have been done singly, as the needs arise and the various steps warrant, and not in one vast grouping. It is wise to draw the basics of the cross section in ink (that is, the raised level, RP, GZ, and SE) while individual points are plotted in pencil and may be erased as necessary to avoid confusion and clutter and thus make room for new points.

Having discerned the correct heights and drop-downs on the cross section, the measurements are transferred to the perspective grid and plotted (fig. 62d). Verify first those objects that overlap other objects. It is

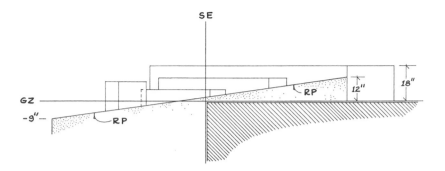

Figure 62c

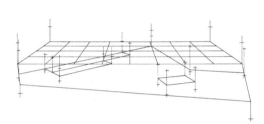

Figure 62d

always safest to verify the downstage furniture (the block) first, then proceed to the steps and finally the larger shape-revealing lines (fig. 62e).

The preceding rake exercises have taken place on slopes that pitch directly downstage. Very often, scenic designs will involve a rake or series of rakes that tip both downstage and to one side. Such angles confront the audience in a **compound** manner, and individual heights must be plotted on one or more cross sections. Accordingly, a thorough study of the preceding exercises and an understanding of how cross sections are used are essential in order to plot both compound rakes and those objects that sit upon them.

There is, however, a shortcut to drawing the bottoms of elements resting on the preceding raked stages. (The tops of the elements must still be drawn using traditional measuring or vanishing point methods.) The following shortcut will work *only if the objects to be transferred rest on a rake that tips exclusively downstage toward the central observation point.* The rake may be either symmetrical or asymmetrical in design, but it must *not* have a **compound** list; otherwise, the following shortcut will not work.

The Perspective Grid

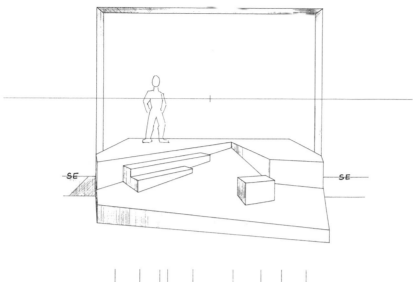

Figure 62e

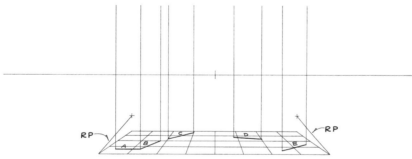

Figure 63a

The perspective grid in figure 63a shows a series of flats (**A–E**) resting on a level stage floor. Along orthogonal 1 (extreme stage right) and orthogonal 7 (extreme stage left) has been drawn the **pitch** of the rake (**RP**). The surface of the rake hits **GZ** at the first transversal and tips up to +15″ at the fourth transversal. The method used to strike in the bottoms of the walls is not at all unlike "Shortcut 2," which involves a "slide over, lift up, slide back" procedure. Referring to wall **A** (which is parallel to an orthogonal) lightly extend its base directly to the left until it crosses orthogonal 1. At this intersection, extend a line straight up until **RP** is crossed and make a mark. From this mark, extend directly right to the vertical edge of **A** and strike a line to the right edge of **A**. This line signifies where the base of **A** rests on the rake (fig. 63b). Repeat

Variations

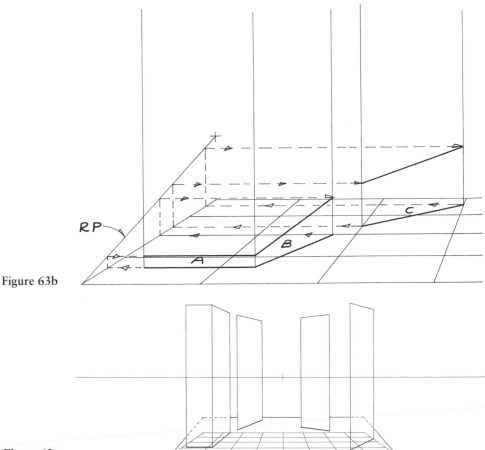

Figure 63b

Figure 63c

this procedure with **B**'s upstage corner and connect the raised-up point to wall **A** so as to complete the base of **B**. Continue with the remainder of units **C–E** (fig. 63c). This shortcut method is ideal in that it eliminates countless measurements and will work for plotting the bottoms of virtually anything resting on a raked surface.

Similarly, the shortcut may be extended for use on the raked thrust. The only real difference in procedure is to "slide over, *drop down*, and slide back." The 1 and 7 orthogonal lines are pulled forward to indicate the extension of ground zero (**GZE**), and below it is drawn the slope of the **raked thrust, RT** (fig. 64a). The floor plans of the benches are drawn

The Perspective Grid

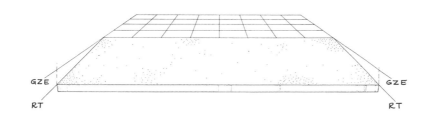

Figure 64a

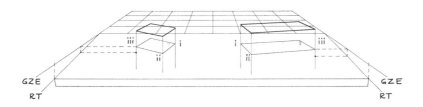

Figure 64b

in, again appearing as if on a level sheet of clear glass protruding from the edge of the level stage floor, and vertical lines are drawn to signify the benches' corners. *Note that the finished heights of the benches are already complete and drawn with heavier lines.* The base of corner **iv** is hidden from view and therefore not of concern. Slide corner **iii** to the right for the larger bench and to the left for the smaller one until crossing **GZE**. Drop down to **RT**, and slide back to cross **iii**'s vertical corner line. This intersection marks the bottom corner of **iii** as it sits on the raked thrust (fig. 64b). Repeat with corners **i** and **ii**. Connecting the dropped-down corner marks **i** to **ii** and **ii** to **iii** will complete the bases of the benches (fig. 64c).

The Two-Point Perspective Grid

The grid examined thus far has been a one-point perspective drawing that has served as an arena for multi-point, scaled renderings. The very

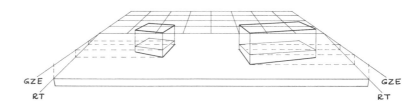

GZE   GZE

RT   RT

Figure 64c

formulation of the one-point grid and the basis for measuring upon it have been specifically related to its single, central vanishing point. Depending on the nature of the theatre's space, the distance of the observation point and the height of the horizon line on the one-point grid can vary and be altered to specific needs. What has remained a constant factor in all of the previous discussions has been the lateral position of the **observation point** (**O.P.**). In all cases, the viewer's line of sight has been centrally located so as to afford an optimum view of the stage space and setting.

Occasionally, a designer may wish to express an alternate view of the stage setting, that is, a viewpoint that is not positioned in the very center of the theatre but, rather, off to the side. An off-center **O.P.** provides an arresting slant to the more traditional central view and is used most effectively to render the predominately thrust-oriented setting and arena staging where the audience partially wraps around the jutting performance space and the placement of scenery must adjust to considerably wider sightlines. (To render a conventional proscenium setting from an off-center **O.P.** would likely be fraught with numerous sightline problems.)

Rendering a setting as seen from an off-center **O.P.** may be achieved in either of two ways. The first way would be to utilize the one-point perspective grid but to change the **O.P.** by gridding the set's floor plan to accommodate the change in view. In other words, orient the first transversal of the floor plan grid (which is actually a bird's-eye view of the picture plane) so as to be parallel to the revised **O.P.** and continue the gridding accordingly.

The second way to render from an off-center **O.P.** is to use the **two-point perspective grid**. The benefits for using the **two-point grid** for the

The Perspective Grid

thrust setting are significant. Most plays staged on thrust and arena stages rely less on scenic units being integrated to the action and more on "open staging" concepts where the action of the play is tied to character confrontations rather than to business requiring doors, windows and other rudiments of realistic environments. Also, if the audience is configured around the thrust stage, sightlines are very open and scenic elements must be placed in arrangements that will accommodate countless viewpoints. A large entrance façade placed at the rear of the acting area is commonly used with the thrust stage, as it provides a substantial background for the vast majority of audience members. The number of required scenic units is greatly minimized and becomes a highly selective process. As such, the stage space is less likely to be infused with numerous, nonessential elements and the complexity of the rendering is reduced. The designer is freer to concentrate on capturing a true emotional environment for the action that can be enhanced immensely by the off-center **O.P.** The presence of *two* vanishing points in the grid also expedites the rendering process.

The visual orientation of the **two-point grid** is more spectacular than the one-point. There is a human tendency, albeit subconscious, to balance and stabilize what is seen. The one-point grid succumbs to this tendency by providing a visual equilibrium, an encapsulated package seeming to exist for the observer's solitary view. The viewpoint offered by the two-point is oblique, as if the observer were really an eavesdropper. The two-point view seems secret and strangely forbidden and is dramatically provocative.

With a uniqueness of perspective comes a certain freedom of expression. Most two-point perspectives, particularly those of an architectural nature, are based on widely separated vanishing points in order to enhance the drawing's realistic impression. Often one or both of the vanishing points will be located far off the drafting board's surface. However, a very effective *theatrical* rendering may be drawn by placing the two vanishing points within reach; if not on the drawing surface, then certainly within the limits of the drafting board. This closer proximity between the two vanishing points will increase the amount of foreshortening but generally not to the detriment of either the rendering's visual intent or the credibility of its proportion. The effect of foreshortening may be minimized by slightly reducing the scale of the rendering. When two vanishing points are located within the drawing surface, a large-scale drawing will feature greater foreshortening than a smaller drawing using the same vanishing points. If the original scale of the rendering was to be ½" = 1'–0", try dropping it to ⅜" scale.

A quick way to draw a **two-point grid** that is very easy and enjoyable to use puts the observation point at an angle 45° from the observation point of the one-point grid. Begin, as usual, by gridding the floor plan of the setting in 2' squares. *Always arrange the gridding so that the number of transversals and orthogonals are even.* Then draw a line from the bottom left corner of the floor plan to the top right corner (fig. 65). This diagonal line will translate on the **two-point perspective grid** as the **base line** (**BL**). To draw the **two-point grid** shown in figure 66:

1. Strike a base line, **BL**. Above the **BL**, at a chosen height, strike the horizon line, **HL**.
2. At the very center of the drawing surface, strike a vertical line. This will establish the point of observation, or the **line of sight**. However, it will also serve as a measuring guide and will be called the **VML**, or **vertical measuring line**.
3. On the gridded floor plan, measure the diagonal of a 2' square (2'-10"). Measure out to the right and left of the **VML** along the **BL** to the number of squares specified on the floor plan.
4. Measure out from **VML** along **HL** as far as possible and to equal distances. These points will become **VPL** and **VPR**, or vanishing points **left** and **right**.
5. From **VPL**, extend lines as necessary through the intervals on **BL**. Repeat with lines from **VPR** to complete the **two-point perspective grid**.

Similar to the manner one would plot on a one-point perspective grid, locating points on the two-point grid is achieved by either visual transfer or by first measuring their counterparts on the floor plan. If, for instance, a wall were to end somewhere within a floor plan square (see **i**, in fig. 67a), one would measure where the end of the wall was in relation with the nearest transversal and orthogonal and extend these points to where the **BL** was crossed (**x, y**). Locate the corresponding transversal and orthogonal on the two-point grid by referring to their 2' intervals marked on **BL**. Measure out either to the right or left from the interval, depending on the location of **i**, and "push back" to **VPL** and **VPR**. Where the "push back" lines cross signifies the position of **i** (fig. 67b).

The Perspective Grid

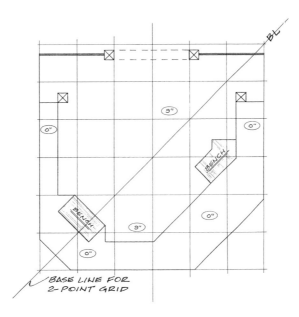

Figure 65

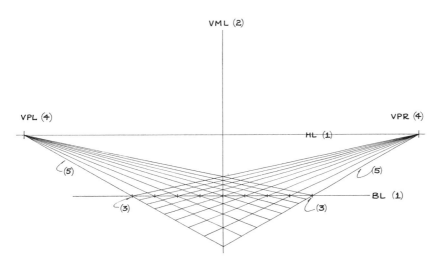

Figure 66

Variations 129

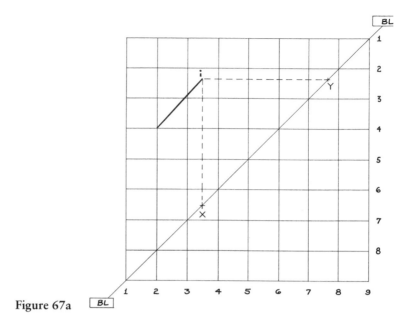

Figure 67a

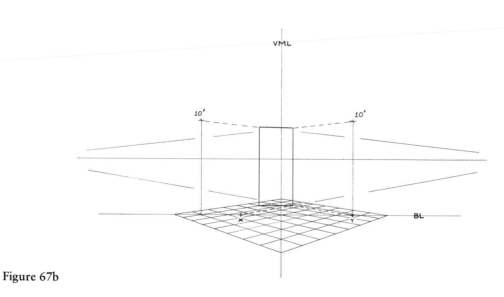

Figure 67b

The Perspective Grid

Figure 68

The **VML** may be measured upon to establish the heights of objects by pushing back or pulling forward lines in association with the vanishing points. Also, wherever **VPL** or **VPR** lines intersect on **BL** is a scaled position, and heights may be measured directly up and down from it, and then pushed or pulled as needed. Figure 68 features a scenic sketch drawn on a **two-point perspective grid**.

6. Coloration and Form

Once the perspective drawing has been verified and all of the notations and supporting lines have been erased, one must now add color, imply texture, and enhance the form of the setting. In short, the perspective drawing now becomes the perspective **rendering**.

Ideally, a theatrical **rendering** is meant to capture a particular moment of the play. Designers should be selective in their choice of scene or moment to render, as the images portrayed can make an overall statement about the setting's support of the play. Some plays cannot help but offer an obvious moment. "The Kiss" from *Cyrano de Bergerac* or the appearance of Banquo's ghost during the banquet scene in *Macbeth* are two such moments that spring to mind; both are significant or pivotal scenes that are full of dramatic import and are visually inspiring. Alas, many plays do not contain scenes with such strong visual imagery. In fact, some settings change little, if at all, during the course of the play and offer a less graphic or stylized visual support than the examples cited. More often than not, during the course of the performance the setting will really not change at all (unless, of course, it is a multi-set show). The lighting, however, *will* most likely change, and therein will lie the key to choosing the moment to render. Whether a scene is brightly lit, swathed in shadow or creased by side lighting is unimportant; deciding which of the scenes is enhanced most by the lighting so as to support the play's most significant moment leads the designer directly to the choice of scene to render.

Varied Backgrounds

The background refers to the drawing and painting surface. Though renderings may be done on a variety of media, the choice of background must be suitable to the techniques to be used in the colorization process. Some designers may prefer using color washes, while others enjoy using richer, opaque colors. Many will simply use whatever background or painting surface supports and defines the techniques and media they wish to employ. With very few exceptions, a **mat**, or nonreflective, surface is the most desirable to use for sketches and renderings. Surfaces that have even a faint sheen will not evenly absorb the color medium (there is always some degree of absorption) and most likely will provide an annoying reflection.

A designer may choose to render on almost any type of paper. Watercolor paper is quite versatile but can be easily torn and may buckle when drying. For sheer durability, illustration board is a popular choice. Consisting of several thin paper layers pressed together and laminated with watercolor paper, the nature of the binding process, be it by cold- or hot-press, will determine whether the board's finished surface is either sleek and slightly reflective (hot-press) or mat (cold-press).

To withstand the transfer process involved when working with a perspective grid and to maintain a lasting drawing and painting surface of quality, **mat board** is a preferable choice of background for the perspective rendering. It is sturdy, able to withstand frequent erasures, and reacts well to washes, markers, and inking pens. Though it will absorb water, the rate of absorption is relatively slow and, accordingly, will allow the artist to puddle and wet blend colors. Warping can be a problem if the board is overly saturated but gluing small wooden stiffeners to the back of the board will eliminate the bow. **Mat board** is used most commonly for matting, or attractively enclosing other works of art within a picture frame. It can be found in a wide range of textures for decorative matting purposes, but it is also readily available in nontextured finishes that accept pencil and pen lines with remarkable ease. **Mat board** is produced in an exhaustive spectrum of shades as its traditional role in framing requires it to complement the color of any work of art with which it comes in contact.

The atmosphere created by a rendering depends greatly on the color and hue of the background. At one end of the color spectrum is black.

Renderings with black backgrounds can be quite provocative. Just as there can be no light without dark, the black background provides the designer with, in effect, a darkened stage. To provide illumination is to add splashes of color or bright-edged silhouettes to scenic forms; and while the visual effect can be quite startling, there is a heavy, enigmatic feel to the rendering due to the overwhelming presence of the black background that may or may not reinforce the designer's intent. The main problem caused by a black background is not one of unintentional mood but rather the difficulty in transfer. Drawing the perspective grid on the black background and transferring onto it is not an easy task. Standard pencils will not be visible and transferring a previously drawn sketch to the black board is quite time-consuming. The best method is to draw with a white pencil, or **blueprint pencil**, but as they are manufactured with fairly soft leads the pencil requires continual resharpening. In addition, white pencils use a "lead" containing paraffin, which when applied heavily will repel water-based paints.

At the other extreme of the spectrum is the white background. The resolution of pencil line, even those lines drawn faintly, is high. There is little to be said against the white background except that few surrounds on the stage are actually white, and therefore, the board must usually be treated with a wash of some color to approximate the surround of the stage. Accordingly, the white background should not be chosen to render a night scene or one that is cloaked in mystery. The artist will spend more time darkening the majority of the painting surface than painting the scenery to appear on it.

The obvious choice of background color lies in the hundreds of hues commercially available between the absolutes of black and white. The carefully chosen background color does more than begin to establish a mood or make a visual statement; it is a foundation for all subsequent colors. However, the degree to which the background is integral to the visual statement is directly related to the choice of color media and the techniques employed.

Color Media

There is no right or wrong medium to use for coloring renderings. Designers use a color medium out of a preference that has evolved through much experimentation and practice. Often designers will combine media: the initial, large effects are achieved through what has become a personally comfortable and efficient medium, while subsequent steps to impart texture or crystallize an object's form often make use of media intended to increase visual impact. While any number of coloring methods may be employed, the following media are the most common to theatrical use.

Colored Pencils

Colored pencils are available in wide ranges of color. What once was a limited color medium has exploded to offer countless hues within the spectrum; however, they do not mix well with one another as do colors in a liquid medium. Too much of a buildup results in a slight sheen. They are handy, though, for imparting subtle, gritty textures over painted areas. They can also be prudently used to highlight edges of moldings and to indicate hotspots caused by bright lighting. Their visual impact is limited; regardless of how many times the rendering is worked the brilliance of the colors can be taken just so far; compared with other media they lack a vibrancy and can never be made to "pop" unless enhanced by another medium. Colored pencils are, however, safe to use: one may be as bold as pencil strokes allow yet still be assured a clean and regimented adherence to straight edges and curved boundaries.

Watercolor Pencils

Watercolor pencils are colored pencils that can be wet with a brush after application. This results in a slight bleeding. They are largely ineffectual, and one would be better to combine washes of watercolor paint with regular colored pencils to achieve a wider range of effects.

Pastels

Pastels come in two forms, the **chalk** variety and the **wax** pastel. The **chalk pastel** resembles blackboard chalk and is available in sets of spectrum colors and extensive monochromatic hues. They are usually found in three degrees of hardness—soft, medium, and hard—but the most vibrant colors are available only in the soft range. **Chalk pastels** blend and intermix well but require a spray fixative to maintain adherence to the drawing surface and reduce the possibility of smudging. As such, **chalk pastels** are not suitable for fine, precise colorization but work well for broad, dramatic strokes. **Wax pastels** contain a wax binder and feel slightly oily. They blend more effectively than their drier chalk counterpart, but their wax base will repel a liquid medium; in order to combine **wax pastels** with a watercolor, the painting step must precede the pastel. A **wax pastel** will stick to paint, but not the other way around.

Markers

Markers are commonly found in "watercolor" form or in semipermanent and permanent ink forms. They are available in a multitude of colors, and feature various tip forms whose degree of hardness will vary depending on the style and make of the product. **Watercolor markers** contain a nonpermanent pigment that flows from the marker quite freely and can be liquified to produce blurred edges or suggestive block fill-ins. Their status runs from temporary to semipermanent and will smudge and run if wet accidentally. As such, **watercolor markers** should not be used for extra-fine lines or intricate detail work but can be used effectively for bolder strokes. **Watercolor markers** combine very well with watercolor paints, pencils, semipermanent and permanent markers. Semipermanent and permanent ink markers are not found in hues as vivid as one will find with **watercolor markers**, though the variety has increased over recent years. Their tips are usually harder than those found on **watercolor markers** and the ink-pigment dries rather quickly and is difficult to blend. Colors may be overlapped but with hard-line distinctions. However, their ability to strike crisp and thin lines make them especially conducive to detailed work. With either type of marker one must proceed the same way one uses dyes: always start with the lightest color and proceed toward the darkest. Once the colors have set they cannot be lightened. Highlighting is achieved by either leaving certain areas untouched or using another medium such as opaque paints to create the brighter areas.

Paints

Paints come in countless premixed colors, can be mixed to create an endless number of additional colors, and combine well with virtually every other medium. For use in rendering the most common forms of paint to be used are:

1. *Watercolor*. Perhaps the most traditional of paints used for theatrical set and costume renderings, **watercolors** are available in dry cake or tubular paste form and dry to a transparency. They are exceptional for painting dreamy and gauzy effects but will not serve well as an opaque medium. The amount of pigment needed, when mixed with water, to create an opacity will cause the paint to dry with an undesirable sheen. **Watercolors** are not permanent and can be reworked.

2. *Gouache, or opaque watercolors*. Highly favored because it is available in colors that closely approximate the colors of actual scene paint, **gouache** is found in cake and paste form. Because it can be mixed to colors that translate well to the stage, **gouache** appears a little less vibrant than watercolors. (Most scene paint is mixed, however, to come to life under stage lighting and therefore tends to be "browned" or "greyed-down" in order not to appear overly bright when lit.) The paste form is initially more expensive but will last longer, is more easily "stretched," and, provided the tube's cap is tightly secured, will not dry out or crack as will happen with the cake form. **Gouache** is liquified with water to be opaque and may be thinned to create clean, transparent washes. It works well on white and black backgrounds, as well as on any other color. It dries to a mat finish and it works well in combination with other media; but its ability to be both transparent and opaque makes it a full-service choice. **Gouache** does not dry to permanence and may be reworked.

3. *Acrylic*. **Acrylics** come in tubular paste form in a wide variety of dynamic colors. They are mixed with water and are worked in much the same way as gouache. A reason not to use **acrylics** is that they will dry to a slight gloss when used as an opacity. On the plus side, while **acrylics** do allow for some initial reworking, they will dry to a permanent, self-protecting finish.

4. *Latex*. **Latex** is not widely used for two reasons. One, it will not easily or uniformly thin down in small quantities to create transparencies. **Latex** is generally used for large jobs, not for items as relatively

small as a rendering. It is more suitable to painting the scenic model where colors can be layered, if need be. Second, **latex** has a tendency to "grey-down" when drying. It looks far more dynamic when wet than when dry. Latex is a choice for some designers, however, as it will closely approximate the numerous settings that are painted with latex paint.

Rendering with Gouache

Rendering with paint takes practice. Paint is a liquid medium applied mostly with a brush, and that may inhibit some designers. They may feel that the brush decides what to do rather than the painter. With a little diligence many come to realize that the brush can become their most eloquent ally: a direct extension of themselves, a true instrument for artistic expression. Of course, every artist needs a little help. Selecting the best possible paint brushes will make one's efforts easier to stimulate.

Of all watercolor brushes available, the ones without equal are made from **red sable.** They are durable yet supple, retain paints, wash generously, come in a variety of shapes and sizes, and are fairly expensive. Some synthetic brushes are available that capture the feel of **red sable,** are more affordable and of good quality, but they must be chosen with care. Most designers carry at least three different-size brushes: one for large background expanses, another of medium size for middle ground fill-in, and a third smaller size for detail lines. While some prefer brushes with round ferules, flat-ferule brushes that resemble miniature scene painting liner brushes are indispensable for striking thin, crisp lines or tapering, curved strokes. Avoid the black bristle brush commonly found with watercolor sets. The best rule to follow is that any brush that comes *with* the paints is bound to be inferior to those sold individually. Experiment with different brushes and always purchase good quality brushes.

With practice, painting with gouache can be a quick and extremely versatile way to color the rendering. At the outset, the designer may elect either of two approaches, though a combination of the **opaque method** and the **wash method** will eventually prove the most serviceable. Of the two, the opaque method is best suited to renderings drawn on a dark background where strong splashes of color are needed for a striking contrast. Obviously, opaque paint is thicker than a wash and consequently, does not flow off the brush as easily. This may make detailed strokes more difficult to paint than those made with a thinner mixture. Mistakes made with opaque gouache can be fixed but not nearly as easily as with a wash. Conversely, opaque paint will cause the brush to drag slightly and may aid the designer in keeping within the lines.

Applying paint mixed to wash consistency is freer flowing. The brush glides across the surface with ease. Washes can also be built up to achieve opacity. In general, when creating a rendering using the perspective grid, the **wash method** of colorization is far superior to the **opaque method** for achieving accuracy and crispness, as well as a sense of atmosphere, and is far less time-consuming. Washes nicely overlap lines that have been verified in ink while still allowing the verified lines to show through. This makes the hard-line painting of scenic edges easy to strike. Detail work accomplished during drawing verification can also be easily followed using translucent and transparent washes.

The **wash method** can allow for a greater freedom of painting expression than working with opacities. Gauzy images and bleeding puddles of color may be introduced as expressive design tools (in the same way dyes would be used on the stage). Trying to achieve the same results with opaque colors is futile. Also, colors seem easier to mix and match when used as washes. Light, opaque colors can contain a great deal of white that, when mixed with primaries and other rich colors, can cause any number of subtle and varied tonal values. Whereas if one needed to make a light brown wash, brown pigment may be thinned with water to approach a pale shade, making the entire mixing process markedly simpler, easier to reproduce, and considerably more economical.

However, advocating the wash method puts a great deal of import on the selection of the color for the background or mat board. Washes of paints overlap the color of the mat board; therefore, the mat board color should be carefully selected so as to serve as an appropriate backdrop for subsequent color washes. That is not to imply that using the wash method on a colored background turns the rendering into a monochromatic, but the background should be light enough to draw on yet not be so dominant in color as to inhibit or repel any other colored washes placed upon it. Nearly every stage set has a dominant, or base, color. When using the wash method of rendering, choose a piece of mat board that typifies the intended predominant color but is several shades lighter. If the actual stage set is to be totally painted off-white, the designer must determine what shade of off-white is most appropriate. The answer will be the color of mat board to select as the painting background.

Coloring the rendering involves substantially more than choosing appropriate colors, however. Considerations of **texture, mood,** and **revelation of form** are of paramount importance to ensure the visual propriety of the rendering.

Textures create a largely subconscious reaction in the spectator. Certain textures are soothing and inviting. Others repel intimate touch, evoking little warmth or compassion. As such, on the full-size stage setting, textures can contribute greatly to the establishment of mood. On the theatrical rendering, textures may need to be affected, though usually only a mere suggestion is implied because of the relative size of the rendering. (Texture is not always defined in coarse terms. On the contrary, a sleekness in surface character is textural; the cold, clinical steel and glass of a futuristic setting may speak mountains more than a rough brick fireplace.) Whereas the actual painting strokes used on the full-size setting may be quite broad, too faithful an adherence to the same painting technique on a work the size of a rendering looks comical and ludicrous. Scumbling strokes, when performed on the full-size setting, can create a blotchy appearance. Hues of the same color are mottled together, and depending on the intermingling of the hues and their distance in value from one another, a textural effect is achieved. This scumbling technique reduces nicely to suit the smaller scale of the rendering. However, any subsequent techniques commonly applied to full-size settings, such as the spattering of paint droplets or the stippling use of a sponge, are far too broad and should be avoided.

Creating a sense of **mood** is the result of several influences. The scenic design shapes the visual intent. Types and directions of lines, the mass and size of objects in relation to the actors, texture, color, and illumination are all design tools that play key roles in establishing mood. The extent and selectivity of illumination, that is, what we see and how much, combined with the nature of color are the principal guidelines the designer uses when adding color to the rendering. Creating mood, then, may be said to directly relate to the degree of visibility and the colors that are illuminated. A dimly lit scene surrounded by faint blue light will make a decidedly different statement than the same scene brightly lit by an orange glow.

Revelation of form is another responsibility of the colorization process. A designer may draw an absolutely captivating design only to have its form ignored when the rendering is painted. Much in the same way scene painting must reinforce the shape of the setting by painting darker tones into recessed corners, so, too, must the designer paint the rendering with an acute awareness of the form of the set. Using the wash method alone will not give the verified shape visual form. Areas of the set must be darkened or brightened as the case may be.

To best reveal form, a dominant, or principal, light source must be chosen. Depending on the nature of the design, this source could be anything from a blazing fireplace to a sunlit window to a blinding searchlight. Those surfaces facing the principal light source will be lighter than those facing away from it. The distinction between the amount of illumination given the two surfaces will relate to the time of day, strength of the source, the desired mood, and so forth. Secondary sources may be added but should not overwhelm the impact of the principal light source.

Painting the rendering is, in theory, similar to painting the full stage setting. Certainly, the rendering will not take nearly as long to paint as the actual setting, and the nature of the painting strokes will be simplified, but some of the theories of scene painting can and should be applied to the rendering. For example, scenery is regarded as a supporting element in the production. Though a good set will provide an appropriate environment for the action of the play, focus is almost always geared to the actor. Painting techniques help maintain this focus. The tops of the set are generally painted in darker tones than the bottom, thus directing the eye of the viewer down toward the actor. Also, the values of color on the walls are not so disparate in range as to demand focus but are usually kept within areas of limited contrast so as to do little beyond evoking texture and providing visual propriety. The number of colors is kept to a minimum. Several values of a very few principal colors may find their way onto the setting without creating distracting visual activity. Accordingly, the number of architectural components (for example, bricks) is kept to whatever amount will convey the nature of the construction. These simple rules of scene painting can be transferred with ease to the reduced scale of the rendering.

Figure 69a shows a simple perspective drawing ready to be colored. All unnecessary lines have been erased leaving only those lines that have been verified with ink. As the walls are to be a mushroom brown, a pale tan mat board provides an initial, unifying background color. The principal light source (**PLS**) is the fireplace. Though it is supposed to be quite late at night, the entire set will be slightly illuminated. (Theatre, after all, should not duplicate the real world but rather embellish it to suit its

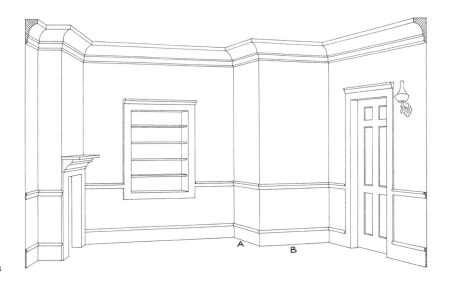

own needs, not to mention those of the lighting designer.) To demon-
strate how two of the walls joined to create a protruding corner (one
wall **A**, facing toward the **principal light source**, while the other, **B**, faces
away from the **principal light source**) are to be painted with **gouache**,
using the **wash method**:

1. The base color for the walls (burnt sienna and sepia) is thinned
    to a translucent wash and applied at the tops of both of the
    walls. Gradually, by adding more water to the brush, the base
    wash is pulled and worked down the walls toward their bot-
    toms. The gradation of consistency will have a direct bearing
    on the impression of a surface texture. Adding inconsistent
    amounts of water and redipping the brush into the base wash
    will result in a mottled appearance, suggesting a surface texture
    such as plaster. Both walls, at this point, are painted with equal
    value, although their tops are painted darker so that the eye of
    the audience will be kept downward and the focus will remain
    on the actor (fig. 69b).
2. Wall **B** faces away from the fireplace and will appear darker than
    wall **A**. Just how much darker depends largely on the time of
    day and the strength of any other sources of illumination. The
    original base wash is deepened to create a **shade wash 1** (in this
    case with a little more sepia), thinned and applied to the top

Coloration and Form

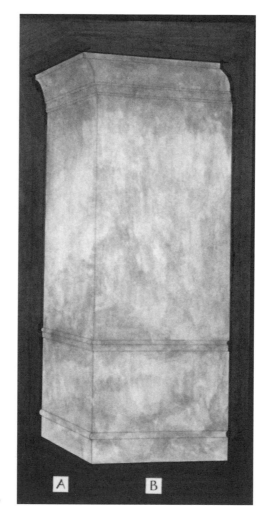

Figure 69b

and worked out from the right recessed corner, or the right edge of wall **B**. Using a little more water on the brush the **shade wash 1** is worked out toward the left edge of wall **B**. The recessed corner (which would exist between wall **B** and the adjacent wall in which the door is cut) should appear darker than the protruding one, but to reinforce the arrangement of the two walls there must be a marked difference in the value of the surface washes of the walls where they meet at the protruding corner. Accordingly, the illusion of the protruding corner of wall **A** is easily

Coloration and Form 143

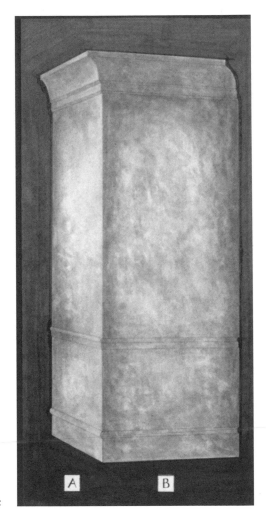

Figure 69c

strengthened by adding a weak tint wash in a hard line and then blending out to the left (fig. 69c).

NOTE: be sure not to have too much water on the brush. Red sable brushes, and their more moderately priced imitators, are able to retain quite a bit of water. After dipping the brush in water, press it lightly and briefly to a paper towel or tissue. If there is too much water already on the painting surface gently squeeze out the brush and apply it to the surface. The brush will draw up the excess and likely create an interesting painting effect!

Coloration and Form

3. **Shade wash 1** may be used on wall **A** as the shade color for the molding. Note that the shade wash is applied to the underside of the protruding molding as if the **PLS** were coming from above and to one side. This was done to simplify the painting example in order to clarify the role the wash plays in creating a basic three-dimensional illusion. In painting the actual rendering, the direction of the **PLS** (the fireplace) would be reversed and emanate from the *bottom* rather than the top. A slightly darker version of this shade wash (**shade wash 2**—add a pinpoint more sepia) should be used for the molding shade on wall **B** (fig. 69d).

A **tint wash** must now be made whose purpose will be to add further dimension to the moldings on walls. For wall **A**, the base color wash is lightened by adding a speck of white.

NOTE: A tint, whether opaque or a wash, does not have to be created using only white. The color of the tint should reflect the color of the light emanating from the **principal light source**. For example, if a full moon is the **principal light source**, start out with some white and then add a drop of blue to simulate the moon's slightly cool glow. By contrast, if the moon were a "harvest moon," substitute the blue additive with a pinch of orange.

Add a little water to thin the **tint wash**. It is always better to have a **tint wash** that is too thin rather than too thick. Mixing white into a previously mixed wash will really "pop," as the white tends to cast over, or create a film, as it dries. A nicely thinned **tint wash** will glaze nicely to a translucency, and if it does not read strongly enough, another application will quickly increase its opacity.

4. Keeping in mind the shapes of the moldings, apply the **tint wash 1** to wall **A**. In order to reinforce the position of wall **B** as facing away from the **PLS**, mix up a second **tint wash 2** with the base color wash used for wall **B** and apply to **B** (fig. 69e). A tint of a tint, or **flash**, may be introduced here to give added "pop" to a molding on wall **A**.

5. Finally, a **shadow wash** is added to reinforce protruding elements. The **shadow wash** is a totally translucent wash that, when applied in a single stroke alongside a shade line and away from the **PLS**, represents a cast shadow and allows previous painting steps to show through (fig. 69f).

Figure 69d

Walls **A** and **B** have been painted as an isolated exercise. While the basic illusions of a protruding corner and applied moldings have been achieved, the painting has no character, sense of atmosphere, or mood. The two walls are detached. Not only is the **principal light source** (if there is one) matter-of-fact, its point of origin is incorrect; nor is it shown or implied in any way. In order for the two walls to come to life, they must be shown in their respective places with the rest of the setting, and illuminated so as to reinforce the **principal light source**. The **principal light source** is not always shown on the rendering. Often it is sug-

Coloration and Form

Figure 69e

gested and not seen, although its effects can be seen. A light piercing down through a skylight or slicing up through floor bars or pulsating from an offstage location is an example not only of an unseen **principal light source** but also of the mystery, intrigue, and sense of isolation that it can create.

Walls **A** and **B** are replaced into the rendering, and "lighting" them according to the **principal light source** (the fireplace) automatically affords them a role (fig. 70). Just as one actor needs another for conflict, reinforcement, or change, so, too, are walls **A** and **B** affected by the

Coloration and Form   **147**

Figure 69f

shapes of things around them. Shadows are cast and elongated; corners are deepened; and highlights are brushed with the glowing color of the (in this case) roaring fire. For visual and dramatic interest, a **secondary light source** (the wall sconce) has been added. Note that this secondary source has a moderate effect on the protruding planes near to it. Its brightness in no way matches the power of the fireplace, so, accordingly, it does not steal from the rich atmospheric contribution made by the fireplace. Though this rendering, at first glance, might appear complex and overwhelming to the novice painter, the steps involved in its paint-

148   *Coloration and Form*

Figure 70

ing are no more difficult than the steps used to paint walls **A** and **B**, above:

1. Choose an appropriate background (**mat board**) color.
2. Draw the **perspective grid** and all aspects of the setting in pencil (2H hardness works well).
3. **Verify** lines in ink: 0.1 or 0.2 nib, permanent ink. Erase all lines not verified.
4. Mix the predominant set color(s). Thin to a wash and experiment on extra pieces of the same **mat board**.
5. Paint what is furthest away *first*, and work downstage toward the observer.
6. Mix a **shade wash** of the predominant color(s) and apply to areas not facing the **PLS**. This step creates the set's **revelation of form**. Varying the nature of the brush strokes in this step creates a mottling of tones and lends an impression **texture**.
7. Moldings and paneling are treated with **tint, shade**, and **shadow washes**.
8. Three-dimensional wall arrangements are given added form revelation, while increasing the brilliance and shadows caused by the **PLS**. **Tint washes**, made from the base color wash of the

walls, are added to the those walls and protruding corners that face the **PLS**.

9. Deeper **shade washes** and **shadow washes** are applied to indicate how overlapping objects relate to the **PLS**.

10. **Flash washes** are applied to the moldings and are added on top of some areas of **tint washes** for dramatic emphasis and to contrast shadows cast using the **shadow wash**. This creates a suggestion of **mood**.

On exterior or interior settings that contain a fair amount of wood, lightly coloring with a colored pencil *after the washes have dried* will impart a nice textural feeling and can be regulated to suggest graining and dry brushing. The colored pencil must be applied sparingly so as to act as a dry glaze over the washed background. Do not apply to such an extent that a sheen results.

Rendering Examples

Using gouache, particularly in the form of the wash method, is the most desirable medium for coloring the perspective grid rendering, particularly when a large amount of intricate detail must be shown. But as much as one may praise the advantages and qualities of the wash method, another will swear by an alternate method, claiming it to be the most reliable and effective. The process of rendering and the manner and technique of colorization are individual choices based on experience, experimentation, and desired effects. One thing is certain, however, regardless of which medium or technique is selected, rarely does a rendering make use of only one medium or technique. Often, a contrast in mediums will lend a quality or added touch that simply could not have been achieved by the rendering's dominant medium. Wash overlays and colored pencil scratchings on opaque foundations, watercolor markers bled with water and accentuated by pastel, and permanent markers used to define puddled shapes of watercolor wash are but a few of the many common examples of mixed-media techniques. The main rule in rendering technique is that there are no rules. There is not an incorrect method or procedure, only those that better suit one's artistic goal than others.

Coloration and Form

Figure 71

Each of the renderings shown in figures 71–82 makes use of varied techniques and media, while all were drawn on the perspective grid and verified with ink. Note that on many of the examples, several of the darkened areas were given an effect of ambient light and were lightly touched with a colored pencil to help reveal form and slightly enliven what would normally be flat, dead areas. Of the following, only *The Changing Room* was a strict proscenium style setting. All of the others incorporated some type of thrust and raked stages. (All designs and renderings are by the author.)

Dreaming and Duelling (fig. 71), aside from the cyclorama, is painted almost exclusively with opaque gouache; background of light buff mat board.

By contrast, *The Doctor in Spite of Himself* (figs. 72a, 72b) is a stylized design painted with washes of gouache so as to allow a maximum amount of hard-edged inking to show through. Opaque gouache was used for the side masking. Background was a light peach mat board, as the entire set was done in browns backed by an orange colored sky. The symmetrical thrust was topped by curve-edged platforming, while the elevations for the different settings were also predominantly symmetrical.

The rendering for *Lysistrata* (fig. 73) was colored on an off-white mat board background using opaques and washes of gouache. Much of the marbled *orkestra* and the buildings of the *Acropolis* were done with washes, while the entrance to the acropolis, or *propylaea*, repre-

Figure 72a

Figure 72b

sented the last bastion of male dominance and was therefore painted with sturdy, opaque colors.

Our Town (fig. 74) and *Jesse and the Bandit Queen* (fig. 75) were done on bond paper and colored using colored pencils. Darker areas were enhanced with permanent markers.

The amount of available production time can, unfortunately, be a factor that determines both the method of rendering and the extent of colorization. When time is particularly tight, some drawings must be shaded with pencil and, consequently, become scenic sketches rather than renderings. *My Sister in This House* (fig. 76) and *The Red Lion*

Coloration and Form

Figure 73

Figure 74

(fig. 77) were designed when preproduction time was at a premium. Both were drawn on white bond paper. When sketches such as these cannot be colored, some indication (for example, a color flow chart or swatches) *must* accompany the pencil drawing to indicate intended colors. Each of these was shaded lightly with an HB pencil.

The Changing Room (fig. 78) was initially drawn on black mat board with faint white pencil lines and later painted with opaque gouache. An interesting effect of light source was performed on this rendering. As the time of day was to be dusk the **PLS**(s) were the hanging locker-room

Coloration and Form   153

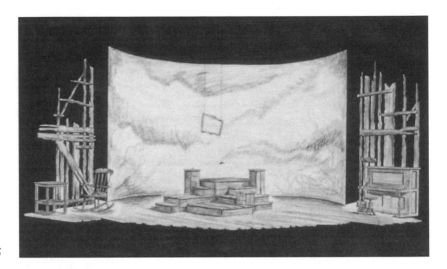

Figure 75

Figure 76

lights. Rather than being painted with rays of light coming from these sources, the rendering was first deliberately painted in tones lighter than would normally occur during the specified time of day. After the rendering was dry, it was laid on a flat surface and cardboard shapes representing rays of light were placed in position on top of the rendering. From a few feet away *black spray paint* was dusted in the direction of the rendering so that a fine mist would fall upon it. The cardboard pieces

154   *Coloration and Form*

Figure 77

Figure 78

were gently removed and the lighter, unsprayed areas of the rendering showed through as a striking illusion of hanging light sources.

Act 1 of *An Enemy of the People* (fig. 79) was drawn on tan mat board and colored almost exclusively with permanent markers. The only deviance was the settee (to the right of center), which was painted in opaque gouache because background verification lines were inked by accident before the settee was verified.

Our Country's Good (fig. 80) used a light seaweed colored mat board background. The sky area was watercolor wash; the ship's skeleton was

Figure 79

Figure 80

opaque gouache; and the remainder was done with combined gouache washes.

The rendering for *The Dining Room* (fig. 81) was intended to be inviting and exude a soft and timeless elegance. As such, the colors were kept to warm, yet pale earth tones and were applied in well-thinned washes. The background color of pale mushroom-colored mat board was especially integral to the painting, as some areas were left virtually unpainted. The detail of the furniture pieces was able to show through and was lightly accented with tints and shades, thus serving as a prime example for the propriety of using the wash method.

Coloration and Form

Figure 81

Figure 82

Lastly is the rendering for *Salt-Water Moon* (fig. 82), a Canadian comic-drama dealing with the reunion of young lovers. The mood is one of romance: a pleasant evening in some August of the 1920s on the charming shore of Newfoundland. The presence of the moon, reflected on the sea, is an essential component in the whimsical light of the evening. The house, porch, and stylized road below it were painted with combinations of opacities and washes, while the moon, its reflection on the water, and elements of the two characters were given added import and painted with opaque gouache. The background was a light Prussian blue mat board.

Coloration and Form   157

It must be stressed that to be able to paint and have the confidence to experiment and develop varied abilities in the process take practice. Though it is quite possible to become adept in a very short time at drawing the perspective rendering, colorization is another matter. Regardless of the method one chooses, coloring the rendering is a far more expressive step than the drawing and inking stages of the process. Painting is restricted only to the extent of its physical boundaries. Within the scaled parameters lies a limitless space for personal style and artistic expression. The development of a style that has a uniqueness of expression is a timeless, ever-changing journey that can only be traveled by the eager and devoted student.

7. Presentation

The auditorium lights fade to black, the music swells, and the stage lights begin to glow and slowly come up. All attention is focused on the stage. Aside from individual feelings of anticipation and wonder, these beginning cues have, in their purpose, done nothing more than capture one's attention and direct it to a specific area: the stage. Whereas a moment ago the auditorium was illuminated, now it has darkened and all heads turn to the stage. The simple transition from unfocused to directed attention was achieved by **selective visibility**. Not unlike a moth, it is only normal that one is attracted to the light within a darkened space.

Viewing the rendering is not usually done in a darkened room, but a certain amount of selective visibility is essential in order to concentrate upon it. The designer must first direct attention to the rendering by darkening or blackening all that is nonessential. Each of the finished renderings shown in figures 71–82 was surrounded by darkness. The tops, bottoms, and sides of the renderings were painted either black or a very dark color appropriate to the main color scheme of each rendering. Therefore, any area of the stage not containing an element of scenery (or anything not intended for focus) was darkened. In this way, the designer attempts to direct attention to important elements and prevent the eye, within reason, from wandering. In some renderings, the set may appear to gradually fade into the darkness, while in other examples a hardline distinction between the edge of the scenery and darkness is maintained. Either way, the purpose behind darkening the nonessential is one of selective visibility, or direction of focus.

The **presentation** of the rendering is nearly as important as the rendering itself. An appropriate, attractive packaging cannot help but heighten the efforts of the designer and further indicate the extent of his or her artistry, preparedness, and professionalism.

Protection and Framing

Even though some media (specifically, indelible markers and acrylics) dry to a near permanent (if not totally permanent) state, protecting every rendering against spillage and other accidents is essential. Renderings can become works of art and, as such, should be treated for longevity and future enjoyment.

Protecting the face of the rendering is of paramount importance. If done with pencils or pastels, the rendering can be "fixed" with a type of aerosol fixative. Following the instructions carefully on the can, a spray fixative will prevent the pencil and chalk from smudging. Overspraying may result in a slight sheen, cause bond and tracing paper to warp and crinkle, or cause a noticeable darkening of colors. Several light sprayings separated by drying periods is preferable to a single, heavy spraying.

Watercolor, gouache, and watercolor marker renderings should not be sprayed for fear of overspraying and liquifying the colors. Instead, cover the surface with **clear acetate**. Acetate is available in a variety of thickness and strengths. Normally, art supply stores offer rolls of acetate designed for graphic artwork, and when attached to the artwork is smooth and wrinkle-free. Avoid any type of clear pastic that can be stretched or wrapped around edges of mat board. Clear acetate is meant to be used as a flat sheet and therefore is fairly stiff in nature and will neither bend easily nor fold. It should also be used to protect acrylic and permanent ink marker renderings, as well as pastel and pencil renderings after they have been "fixed." Clear acetate not only protects the surface from moisture but nicely dresses up the rendering by providing a glasslike appearance.

Further protection for the rendering and enhancement of appearance are achieved by **framing** the rendering. Not to be confused with the wooden frames used for standard picture framing, a frame of mat board is placed over the acetate-covered surface. This frame not only masks nonessentials and supports the notion of selective visibility but also encapsulates and presents the rendering in a clean and aesthetic manner. The color of the mat frame is important as it should enhance the rendering without detracting from it. Accordingly, avoid using the same mat board for the frame as was used for the background. Its light tone will pull the eye outward. Rather, select a mat board whose color is several values darker than the background color. When framed, the rendering will still be thin enough to fit easily into a designer's portfolio for transport.

To Protect and Frame the Rendering for Presentation

1. Cut off excess mat board. (If the rendering was done on paper, trim the excess and mount on a piece of mat board for rigidity.) Though there is no hard and fast rule, allow 1¼" to 1½" of darkly painted mat board on each of the rendering's four sides (fig. 83a).
2. Measure the frame. Again, there is no solitary formula used to determine the frame's size. The *inside* of the frame usually looks nice if it is placed ½" into the four sides of the rendering's darkened surround. Figure 83b is a sketch that indicates a rendering trimmed according to step 1, above. Thin white lines have been

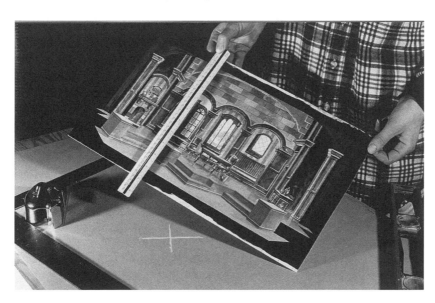

Figure 83a

Figure 83b

added within the darkened surround of the sketch in order to suggest where the inside of the frame will be placed, that is, ½" into the darkened areas on the four sides of the rendering. The *width* of the frame may vary depending on the size of the rendering. Too wide a frame draws unnecessary attention to itself, while too narrow a frame may cause the rendering to appear flimsy. For this example a 2" wide frame was cut. Rendering measurements are taken from right to left scenic edges and from bottom to top scenic edges, in this instance measured at 10½" high by 16" wide. One inch is then added to each of these two dimensions to ensure that the frame's inside edge, when cut, will be equally placed ½" into the darkened surround. Accounting for the fact that the frame was to be two inches wide, four more inches were then added to the two dimensions, thus arriving at the outside dimensions of the frame: 15½" high by 21" wide.

3. Cut the overall outside size of the frame.
4. Measure the inside edges of the frame. Turn the mat board frame over and measure 2" in from its outside to locate and mark with pencil the four inside corners of the frame (fig. 83c). Cutting on the back surface of the mat board will eliminate any marring of the visible front surface.
5. Cut the frame opening. A beveled cut, such as one would see on standard picture frame matting, adds a nice professional look to the frame. This cut can be made for a nominal price at a

Presentation

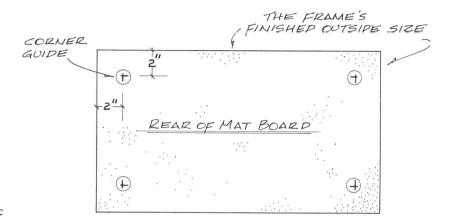

THE FRAME'S
FINISHED OUTSIDE SIZE

CORNER
GUIDE

2"

2"

REAR OF MAT BOARD

Figure 83c

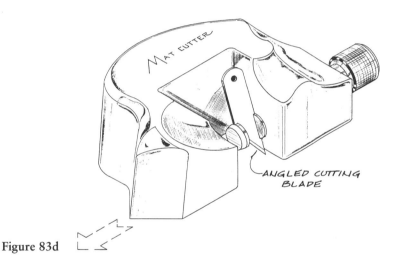

MAT CUTTER

ANGLED CUTTING
BLADE

Figure 83d

picture-framing or art supply store, or made at home by using a handheld cutter such as the commercially available *Dexter Mat Cutter* (fig. 83d). The cutter's blade can be angled and its length can be adjusted to merely score the surface or to cut completely through the mat board. To cut through the mat board frame, the blade is adjusted to protrude below the bottom of the cutter and pierce a sample piece of mat board by approximately 1/32". Place a scrap piece of mat board under the frame to protect the cutter blade. The cutter is placed approximately 1/16" outside

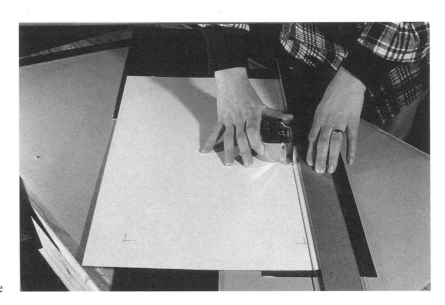

Figure 83e

of the corner marking, and the blade is inserted through the mat board. A straightedge is placed up against the left-hand edge of the cutter and the cutter is then pushed along the straightedge to where the next corner is overrun by approximately 1/16" (fig. 83e). After the first cut rotate the mat board counterclockwise one-quarter turn, pierce the mat board, align the straightedge, and make the next cut. Continue with the remaining two sides of the frame's opening. The inside piece of mat board should easily lift out, leaving an attractively beveled frame (fig. 83f).

6. Cut a piece of clear acetate and attach to the frame. Cut the acetate to a size approximately 1" longer and 1" wider than the opening of the mat board frame. The acetate, when placed on the rear of the frame, should overlap each of the four inside edges of the frame by ½". Carefully tape the acetate to the rear of the frame. Clear or masking tape may be used (fig. 83g).

7. Clean the acetate. With a lint-free cloth, clean the rear surface of the acetate, as it will be applied directly to the surface of the rendering; thoroughly remove all dust particles and fingerprints.

8. Attach the rendering to the frame. Place two pieces of masking tape on the back of the rendering at its top and bottom edges. Extend about 1" beyond the edges. Lay the rendering faceup so

Presentation

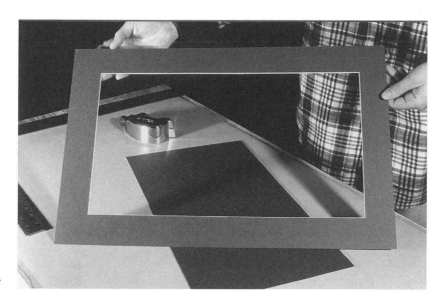

Figure 83f

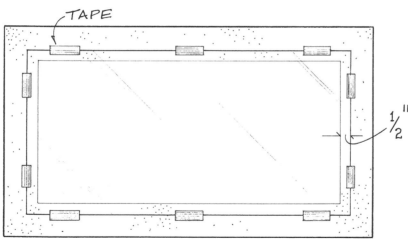

TAPE

½"

Figure 83g

that the sticky surface of the tapes face upward (fig. 83h). Place the frame in place so that an equal amount of darkened surround is seen within all four inside edges of the frame and press down on the frame firmly enough to engage with the tape (fig. 83i). Carefully turn the rendering and frame over as one and press the tapes firmly against the back of the frame. After check-

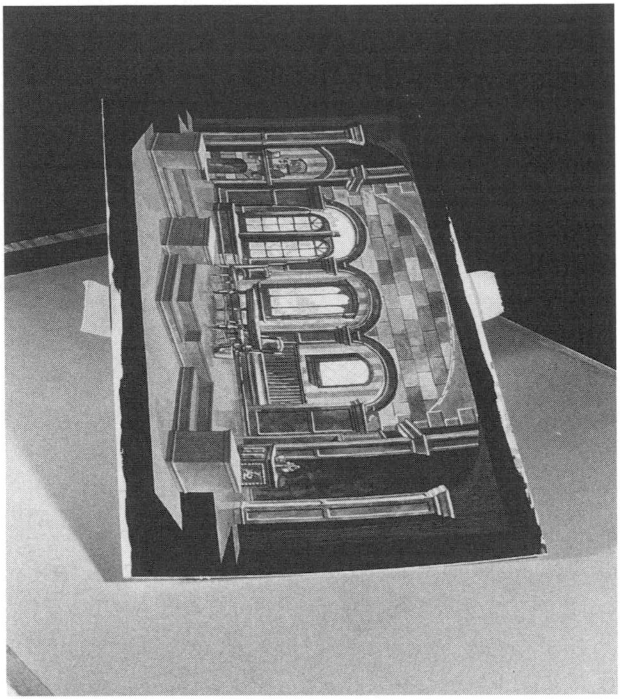

Figure 83h

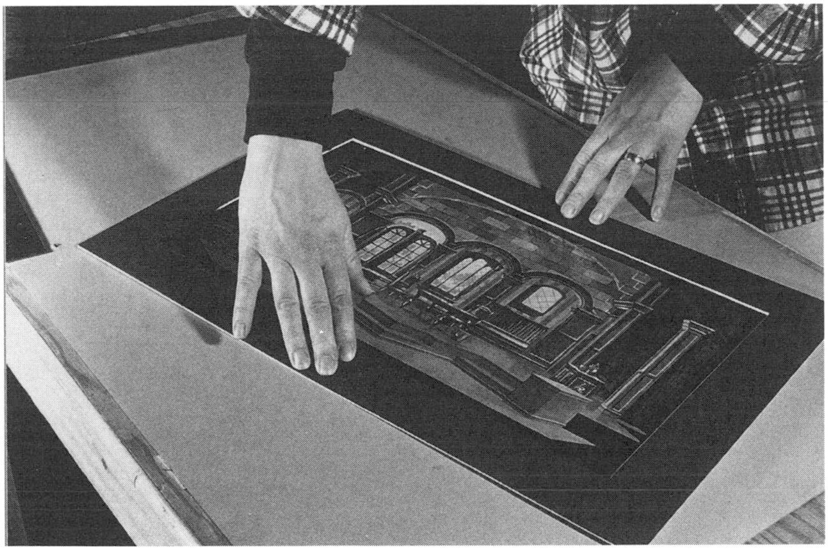

Figure 83i

ing to ensure that the rendering is centered within the opening of the frame, further secure the rendering to the back of the frame with a sturdy tape, such as **duct tape** (fig. 83j).

9. Clean the front surface of the acetate. Lightly spray a paper towel with a mild window cleaner and carefully clean the surface of the acetate.

The mounting and framing of the rendering are now complete, and the rendering should be labeled for presentation. Traditionally, either a self-stick label is attached to the frame or the designer will print the specifics of the production directly onto the face of the frame (fig. 83k).

Duplication and the Portfolio

Freelance designers are commonly asked by prospective employers to submit a portfolio or some form of examples of their work. Many times, portfolios are presented during an interview, but occasionally the portfolio or a part thereof may need to be sent in advance of the interview as part of a screening process. Whatever the situation, it behooves designers not only to maintain an updated portfolio but also to have

copies of their work available should various employment prospects and interviews overlap.

A thorough portfolio should contain examples of both *intended* and *realized* work. Intended work reflects the design and conception process and may be shown through drafting and research sketches, but most commonly is evidenced through renderings or scenic models. Realized work is commonly shown through photographs and slides of the finished product.

It is not necessary that the portfolio be filled with original artwork. Some examples of past work may literally be of priceless personal value to the designer, or at least treasured enough that jeopardizing their quality through mailing or shipping is out of the question. In such instances, replacing the original with a reliable copy made directly from it will suffice for portfolio presentation. A few original renderings and sketches should be included for close scrutiny, but much of the work may be represented by accurate and faithful duplicates.

By far, the best way to reproduce a color rendering is to have a **laser print** made of it. Any other type of quick photocopying is markedly inferior and should be avoided. The **laser printer** resembles a large, extremely sophisticated photocopier. The colors on the laser print copy may be adjusted to closely resemble those on the original rendering or can be altered to various tonal values. The size of the print may also be modified, enlarged, or reduced as needs dictate. The resulting paper print may then be protected, matted, and framed as the original was, and used for circulation or inserted in the portfolio. Laser prints can also be laminated for durability and protection, much in the same way certain restaurant menus are treated with a plastic coating.

Laser print copies may be made from any paper, photograph, or transparency original. The largest original that can be copied for laser printing is 11" by 17". Excellent prints can also be made from color slides and enlarged for ease in viewing. With laser-print copying, the designer can display a laser copy of a rendering alongside a laser copy made from a slide of the finished set. *Whenever possible, the slide of the set should be taken from the same distance and height as were used to draw the rendering's perspective grid.* In this way, the designer's ability to carry design intentions through to realization is showcased, and the designer's credibility is enhanced.

The ideal portfolio case is one with easily removable, protected pages or individual components that may be removed from the case and passed around. Most portfolio cases also feature large inside pockets into which various two-dimensional products can be placed. Interviews or portfolio reviews during which a number of people must crowd around a table to view the artwork or hold slides up to a window is a situation that generally will not bode well for the average applicant. It therefore behooves the designer to arrange the portfolio in such a way that individual items are self-contained and may be conveniently circulated. A few (8–10) slides should be included if a viewer or projector is known to be available but the majority of the designer's work must appear on a scale that can be comfortably and pleasingly seen by the naked eye.

While there is no hard rule as to how much should be included in the portfolio, it is important to avoid redundancy. One should attempt to showcase a variety of design styles and venues. A few examples of the same type of set (for example, a realistic or box set interior) may be included provided that the rendering style, medium, or other significant visual approaches clearly furnish both a visual and interpretative variety.

Also, any related design abilities beyond those that are showcased through renderings, models, drafting, and such, may be included. Examples might include demonstrated abilities in wood working, painting, property construction, or upholstery and fabric manipulation. Any additional work by the designer that has been formerly recognized, copyrighted, or reprinted for authorized publication (books or articles)

Figure 84

should as be included as conveniently as space will provide. The above examples of related abilities are normally placed in secondary areas of the portfolio (such as in a case's large inside pocket) and should, therefore, not eclipse the primary reason why the portfolio is being shown.

The manner in which the material is presented should reflect the quality and the care taken to create the work itself. In order to master the art of perspective rendering, one must be diligent and thorough and must possess a love for drawing and painting. The amount of effort connected with theatrical rendering can be considerable, and the finished product does not occur through serendipity but rather is the result of numerous drawing and coloring steps. The process can be a lengthy one, and it is only appropriate and important that the completed rendering be showcased as befitting both the efforts and the talents of the designer. Convenient, clean, and organized packaging is essential in professional portfolio presentation and will indicate much about the working habits, discipline, and ideals of the designer. Attention to detail is not only crucial to successful scenic design and accurate perspective rendering for the theatre, but is also germane to the attractive presentation of talent (fig. 84).

References
Index

References

Alberti, Leon Battista. 1956. *On Painting*. Translated by John R. Spencer. New Haven: Yale University Press.

——. 1965. *Ten Books on Architecture*. Translated by James Leoni. Edited by Joseph Rykwert. London: Alec Tiranti.

——. 1972. *On Painting and Sculpture*. Edited and translated by Cecil Grayson. London: Phaidon Press Ltd.

Battisti, Eugenio. 1981. *Brunelleschi: The Complete Works*. London: Thames & Hudson.

Bieber, Margarete. 1961. *The History of the Greek and Roman Theatre*. Princeton: Princeton University Press.

Clark, Kenneth. 1969. *Civilisation: A Personal View*. New York: Harper & Row, 1969.

Coulin, Claudius. 1983. *Step-by-Step Perspective Drawing*. Translated by John H. Yarbrough. New York: Van Nostrand Rheinhold.

D'Amelio, Joseph. 1984. *Perspective Drawing Handbook*. New York: Van Nostrand Rheinhold.

Dubery, Fred, and John Willats. 1983. *Perspective and Other Drawing Systems*. New York: Van Nostrand Rheinhold.

Edgerton, Samuel Y., Jr. 1976. *The Renaissance Rediscovery of Linear Perspective*. New York: Harper & Row.

Euclid. *Optics*. 1886. Edited by J. L. Heiberg and H. Menge. Leipzig.

Gadol, Joan. 1969. *Leon Battista Alberti: Universal Man of the Early Renaissance*. Chicago: University of Chicago Press.

Gill, Robert W. 1975. *Creative Perspective*. London: Thames & Hudson.

Ivins, William M., Jr. 1973. *On The Rationalization of Sight*. New York: Da Capo Press.

Jones, Frederick H. 1986. *Interior Architecture: Drafting and Perspective*. Los Altos, Calif.: William Kaufman.

Kubony, Michael. 1986. *The Psychology of Perspective and Renaissance Art*. Cambridge: Cambridge University Press.

Little, Alan M. G. 1971. *Roman Perspective Painting and the Ancients*. Kennebunkport, Maine: Star Press.

Pinnell, William H. 1987. *Theatrical Scene Painting: A Lesson Guide*. Carbondale: Southern Illinois University Press.

Plato. *Republic*. 1941. Translated by Francis MacDonald Cornford. London: Oxford University Press.

Plutarch. *Lives*. 1909. Translated by Dryden and A. H. Clough. New York: Hearst's International Library Co.

Stamp, Gavin. 1982. *The Great Perspectivists*. New York: Rizzoli International Publications.

Vitruvius. 1960. *The Ten Books of Architecture*. Translated by Morris Hickey Morgan. New York: Dover Publications.

Wickham, G. E. 1967. *Rapid Perspective*. London: Alec Tiranti.

Wright, Lawrence. 1983. *Perspective in Perspective*. London: Routledge & Kegan Paul.

Index

William H. Pinnell has designed and painted more than one hundred and twenty major productions in Canada and the United States and has toured extensively as a performer with the U.S.O. In addition to designing, he has directed several productions that have received critical acclaim at the Edinburgh International Festival Fringe. A graduate of the Hilberry Classic Repertory Company at Wayne State University, Pinnell is currently an associate professor of drama at the University of Windsor in Ontario, Canada. He is also the author of the textbook *Theatrical Scene Painting: A Lesson Guide*.